The first insider's view of Kinchela Aboriginal Boys Home, and an important insight into the brutality of the New South Wales government's policy of assimilation.

Dr Gordon Briscoe

This is a frank 'insider's' story of a stolen child who becomes an angry addicted young man and then through a life-changing conversion, the compassionate pastor of his people on The Block, Redfern. Bill Simon tells his story with humanity and hope. It needs to be widely read by Australians as a window into the challenges faced by our indigenous men. I commend Bill for his courage and honesty.

Tim Costello, Chief Executive,
World Vision Australia

Bill said to me once, 'when we came out of Kinchela, the white people didn't want us and our own people didn't know us. We are the forgotten ones'. I hope this book will reveal the great pain and suffering caused to all Stolen Generation men and women and helps us all to heal together.

Pastor Ray Minniecon, Kinchela Boys
Home Aboriginal Corporation

Bill Simon has a heart of gold and a passion to see his people's lives turned around. He speaks with an openness and a passion that touches the lives of others deeply, simply by telling his own story. Read it and be inspired.

Rev. John Macintyre

BACK ON THE BLOCK

BILL SIMON'S STORY

William Simon, Des Montgomerie and Jo Tuscano

For all the members of the Stolen Generations who have passed away.

Aboriginal and Torres Strait Islander people are respectfully advised that this publication contains names and images of deceased persons, and culturally sensitive material. AIATSIS apologises for any distress this may cause.

Contents

Illustrations	vi
Acknowledgments	vii
Editors' note	vii
Foreword	ix
From the storyteller	xii
1. Beginnings	1
2. Stolen	14
3. Lost	63
4. Finding A Way	97
Index	162

Illustrations

Traditional life in the Purfleet region: fishing and hunting. (Haddon Collection/Manning Valley Historical Society)	4
Purfleet Mission Hall and Residence, 1937. (Source unknown)	7
Purfleet Mission schoolchildren with resident missionary Miss Maud Oldrey, 1910. (New South Wales State Archives)	8
Purfleet Mission. (Source unknown)	8
Letter to Aborigines Welfare, July 1957	21
Class at Kinchela Boys' Home. (*Dawn*, August 1965)	25
A dormitory at Kinchela. (*Dawn*, March 1952)	25
Koala drawn by Albert Cooper, aged twelve, resident in Kinchela. (*Dawn*, August 1965)	26
A baptism. (Collection of Bill Simon)	116
Bill Simon outside his house on The Block, 1989. (Collection of Bill Simon)	116
Bill Simon's house, with cross in Aboriginal colours on the balcony, 2008. (Collection of Bill Simon)	119
Bill Simon ministering on The Block. (Collection of Bill Simon)	119
Men performing on The Block. (Collection of Bill Simon)	126
Riot in response to the death of T J Hickey. (Collection of Bill Simon)	145
Demonstration demanding a re-opening of the inquest into the death of T J Hickey. (Collection of Bill Simon)	146
Kinchela reunion, 2002. (Courtesy of Tom Mayne)	149
Sorry Day, 2008. Bill Simon meets Kevin Rudd. (Collection of Bill Simon)	155
Bill Simon and his mother Grace Simon in 1996. (Collection of Bill Simon)	157
Bill and Murray Simon in 1975. (Collection of Bill Simon)	158
Bill Simon and his daughter Vicky on The Block. (Collection of Bill Simon)	159
Bill Simon in front of posters: Kinchela Boys' Home: 'Why', and Sorry Day, 2008. (Collection of Bill Simon)	160

Acknowledgments

The authors would like to thank the following people: Des Simon, the Simon family, Colin Davis, Harold Little, Tom Mayne of World Vision Australia, Ray Minnicon of World Vision Australia, Maurie Garland, photo curator of Manning Valley Historical Society, Manning Valley Shire Council, Julie Welsh, Mark Eddlebuttle, Deborah Tobias, Carol Montgomerie, Frank Tuscano, Dr Gordon Briscoe, and the staff at Aboriginal Studies Press

The authors have made every effort to trace copyright in the images reproduced here. We would be grateful if any copyright holders who have not been acknowledged could contact us care of Aboriginal Studies Press.

Editors' note

Passages in *italic* type have been added by the editors.

Sources

The authors accessed the following sources from which material is cited in the text:

Human Rights and Equal Opportunity Commission, *Bringing Them Home: Report of the National Inquiry into the Separation of Aboriginal and Torres Strait Islander Children from Their Families*, 1997 (available on line at http://www.humanrights.gov.au/Social_Justice/bth_report/report/index.html).

Ramsland, John. 'The Aboriginal School at Purfleet. Part 1: The Development of Segregated Aboriginal Schooling from 1900', *Manning Valley Historical Society Journal* no. 29, November 2006.

Read, Peter, *The Stolen Generations: The Removal of Aboriginal Children in New South Wales 1883 to 1969*, Occasional Paper no. 1, New South Wales Department of Aboriginal Affairs, 1981 (reprinted 2006, available on line from http://www.daa.nsw.gov.au/publications/StolenGenerations.pdf).

Foreword

On 13 February 2008 when Prime Minister Kevin Rudd delivered his historic apology to the stolen generations, he acknowledged that the assimilationist policy of removing Aboriginal children from their families was a stain on Australia's history. In *Back on the Block*, Bill Simon explains why.

There could be no crueller process than removing children from an environment in which they were loved and placing them in one where they are humiliated, physically, emotionally and sexual abused and rarely received affection or comfort. It breaks the spirits of the children who suffer under such a regime. It also breaks the spirits of the parents who, despite their efforts to care and provide for their children, lose them to state institutions.

Through this generous and frank account of his life, Bill Simon illustrates why so many lives were destroyed by the treatment received under state care. His is a story of the horrors and terrors of life at Kinchela Boys Home and it explains why so many boys who were removed from their families and raised in institutions turned into men who were full of anger and devoid of the capacity to love.

Bill's own experiences gave him many emotional issues to deal with. His ability to find a way to come to terms with the impact of his childhood is a heroic story. While Bill is frank about his own personal shortcomings, his mistakes and his regrets, the fact that he was able to transform his self-destructive behaviour and his anger into a life focused on helping others who were less fortunate is inspirational.

Aboriginal culture is one that has a strong tradition of story telling. Bill Simon's account of his life is a gift that follows this tradition. With such an honest telling of his story, remarkably devoid of self-pity but rich in self-reflection, we are shown why it was so important to never forget the stories of the stolen generations and to remember why it was so important for Australia's growth as a nation to acknowledge this great historical wrong.

Bill busts many of the myths created by those who sought to deny the existence of the stolen generations. His story is a stark example of where children were not taken away 'for their own good'. The cruel situation of a father accused of neglect because he was away from the house working to provide for his family is heart wrenching. Bill's family's experience is an example of how parents desperately tried to regain custody of their children and how the system worked against them. Ripped from parents and extended families that loved them and wanted to raise them, children were placed in situations where the neglect and cruelty were such that many reaching adulthood did not recover.

While *Back on the Block* is an inspiration as we watch Bill try to come to terms with how his experiences affected him and dedicate his life to helping others, we also see his path cross many people who were unable to survive the same treatment and live normal lives. Lives shattered by the removal policy litter Bill's story. These anecdotes highlight more than all of the strong legal arguments as to why members of the stolen generation are entitled to compensation. They point to the moral obligation to ensure beyond an apology that compensation be paid for the serious harm suffered by people while children were under the control of the state.

My father, who was also a member of the stolen generations rebuilt his life the same way Bill was able to but he also struggled with the scars from his childhood until the end of his life. When he retired to South West Rocks, I would drive pass the site of the old Kinchella Boys Home on my way to visit him. It is now a retreat to assist those who are coming to terms with substance abuse. The tidy houses — the dormitories are now gone — and the neat lawns conceal the fact that this was a place where many children were brutalised, and their lives shattered along with their self-esteem and self-respect. Looking at the place today, it is hard to comprehend the heartless brutality committed against Aboriginal boys over decades.

Bill Simon, in courageously and so openly telling his story, ensures that we will never be allowed to forget the cruelty of the policy of removing Aboriginal children from their families. He also enables future generations to understand the lasting legacy that institutionalisation and broken families have left on Aboriginal families around the country.

However, there is another precious gift in Bill's story. It is a reminder of the strength of the human spirit and evidence that, no matter how cruel and dehumanising government policies, no matter how tenacious the effort is to assimilate Aboriginal people, there is enough strength and spirit in extraordinary individuals like Bill Simon to ensure that Aboriginal people, our contemporary cultures and communities will continue to resist and survive.

Professor Larissa Behrendt, Professor of Law and Director of Research, Jumbunna Indigenous House of Learning, University of Technology, Sydney

From the storyteller

It is significant that this story was born in water. My mother was from the Biripi Nation, a northern coastal Aboriginal tribal group who have close connections to the sea. Our totem is the shark. We are happiest near the ocean.

In late 1999, I visited Casey's Beach on the south coast of New South Wales when I met Des Montgomerie. We met in the water. I'm a talker. Des is a writer. Standing in the surf, we struck up a conversation and a friendship as well. Friends tell each other their life stories and I told Des mine. I had had little formal schooling and did not have the skills to write down the story of my life. Des offered to write down my memories and so began many years of me talking and Des taping and writing. A few years later, I met Jo Tuscano, also a writer, and Des, Jo and I worked together to bring about the story of my life's journey and work. We decided on a style that fitted the way my life has unfolded, and one that would hopefully keep young people turning the pages, as I want to reach out to them as they travel through the often uneasy years.

This is my story the way I remember it. Telling this story has not been easy. There were times when speaking about my memories caused me great pain. I still have nightmares about the day I was stolen. I didn't see my mother again until well into my thirties, and by that time I had turned into someone that not many mothers would have wanted for a son.

This is a true and accurate account of my life, from childhood to my present age of fifty-six. It is a plain, factual account, written without the usual trappings of descriptive words to enhance the message. I have tried to be thorough and accurate in all recollections, and in so doing, from time to time one may wonder just what it's all about. I am one of the 'Stolen Generations' and my life has been directly affected by that fact right up to the present day. On many occasions my thoughts and actions have been manipulated and determined by my earlier experiences. Naturally this has had a profound effect on my life and much heartache has been caused to me and to so many others who have been a part of my life.

I have covered all stages of my fifty-six years, but because the stolen years were so dramatic and life-changing, I have given a lot of attention to this period in my life. Any semblance of a normal childhood was cut short at the age of ten and I didn't really start to get back on track until I was in my thirties. It is to this period of my life that I have directed extra attention and energies to in this book. Because of the grim circumstances I sometimes encountered as a stolen one, parts of this story will be unsettling for some people, especially those who were a part of the stolen generations. I've changed certain names in order to respect those people who, due to privacy and culture, do not wish to be acknowledged in any way.

I sincerely hope others in the same situation as me will take comfort in the fact that none of us are alone in the pain we feel. All of the ex-Kinchela Boys' Home boys understand and indeed experience that deep and ever-present pain, which wasn't of our making. The deep, distressing pain we feel day in and day out shows itself in so many different ways. Sometimes it's in the form of violence, alcohol and drugs, and other times it is displayed in relationship behaviour. Kinchela men aren't always able to show the love they feel, which is a direct result of our treatment.

Of course it may have been that some of these people who hurt us so much actually believed they were doing the right thing. Maybe the guards thought because they were only following orders they weren't responsible — well, they were wrong. Some of the guards thought they had the right to carry out the injustices with a clear conscience, all because of the colour of our skin and our different way of life. They too were wrong. We all know they were wrong, every fibre of our being tells us that they were wrong.

I am telling this story because it needs to be told. No reason, however well intentioned, will ever justify what happened to us. To say that Aboriginal children were taken away from their parents for their own good is a lie. I was taken over forty years ago, and nothing good has ever come out of that decision.

I ask my brothers and sisters of the Stolen Generations to read my story. It is their story as well. I ask that non-indigenous Australians read my story so that this sad chapter in our history

From the storyteller

may be better understood. My journey through this life has been rocky but I have come to a place where there is no bitterness. Sadness, yes. A sense of injustice, yes.

In Aboriginal culture our totems are there to guide and protect us. And if you believe that all things happen for a reason, then perhaps the shark was guiding me towards Des and Jo so that I could at last tell my story, because, in telling it, it may perhaps lead people to understand what happens when children have no-one to guide them and governments do not protect them at all.

Bill Simon

BEGINNINGS

Mission statement

If you were to ask me if I had a happy childhood, the answer would be a definite yes. I was loved, fed, clothed and cared for not only by my parents but also by our extended family that lived around us. As far as I was concerned, I had no problems. Small children are oblivious to the anxious, hushed voices of their parents late at night, to the complexities of the adult world with all its worries, to the feelings of hopelessness that parents might have when they realise that they cannot offer their children much of a future. Much later on in life, I knew what people probably thought: 'He must have had a rotten childhood. He's ended up like he did because his parents probably neglected him.'

My childhood didn't turn rotten until I was ten. Like the families around us, we lived in a small hut made out of wood and corrugated iron. We had a table, chairs, two beds, a cupboard and a wood stove. There was no electricity and no running water. Behind our house was a dam where we used to catch fish and yabbies, using a bit of string tied to a small empty tin with bait in it. Often these yabbies fed the whole family with Mum's soup as well. I had a normal, poor but very happy Australian family life. Well, almost.

Most Australian families lived in a place of their own choosing, coming and going whenever they felt like it. They went to work, came home, did the shopping and bought and ate what they felt like eating. Not us. We lived on the Purfleet Mission, just outside of Taree in New South Wales. It wasn't a place of our choosing, we couldn't come and go whenever we wanted, there were no jobs to go to, no shopping to do and no decisions about what to buy and eat. All of our food was rationed out, and if the manager was displeased with us our rations could be cut or held back.

*

With colonisation Aboriginal life had changed dramatically. White cedar getters and their convict servants started arriving in the Myall and Manning areas in 1816, dispersing the tribes and having a devastating effect on traditional lifestyle. Settlers arrived in the Manning Valley in 1831, and conditions deteriorated rapidly for the Aborigines. They lost land, sacred sites and hunting grounds as settlers took up land grants. Wildlife dwindled as a result of the settlers' guns, timber-getting and cattle grazing. By 1840 the natural food supplies were almost exhausted. The traditional owners of the land were driven to the fringes of the towns where some people found employment on the railways, farms and cattle stations. A fringe camp was established at Taree, and later, in 1890, an Aboriginal camp was established on Purfleet Station. Originally, the Purfleet Reserve comprised twelve acres, and it was later known as the Purfleet Mission and expanded to an area of 51 acres.

Compulsory education for all children aged between six and fourteen years was introduced in 1880. At first, Aboriginal children enrolled in local schools, but by the mid-1880s there was a policy of educating Aborigines at mission schools. A Mission school and church, run by the United Aborigines Mission, were established at Purfleet Reserve in 1902 and operated for many years.

Purfleet Station was Government Reserve Number 89 and was established in 1900 by the Aboriginal Protection Board (see Ramsland, 'The Aboriginal School at Purfleet', p. 7). It was at one time called 'Sunrise Station', but that name was later dropped because of negative associations with the Japanese flag during the Second World War. The area was known to the Aboriginal people as 'Turrumbumdeen' meaning 'long grass among the trees'. Purfleet, like all government missions scattered all over the country, existed so that Aboriginal people could be kept in the one place, where the government could keep watch over them.

After 1932 Aboriginal people were not allowed to leave the missions without permits, which were only granted to a few 'approved' Aborigines. Some women married white men just to escape from mission life. During the Second World War there was employment for Aboriginal men and some worked off Purfleet but with the end of the war came unemployment and the men had little or nothing to do.

*

The management at Purfleet had no knowledge or interest in Aboriginal culture and so had their own idea of how we should be treated. This was the period of assimilation. Aboriginal culture and heritage was out. White man's culture and laws were in and we had absolutely no say in it whatsoever.

It was into this tumultuous period in Australian Indigenous history that I was born to Isaiah (Ike) Carter and Grace Simon on 30 March 1947. My great-great-grandfather was Chinese and came out in the gold rushes. My father was from the Black Duck Tribe from down near Wallaga Lake, my mother from the Biripi people who inhabited the area between Tuncurry, Taree and Gloucester. The Simon family is one of the oldest families in the district, having been settled there, with four other families, for many generations. Traditionally we spoke a dialect of the Kattang language, a language that apparently is spoken twice as fast as English. The name Taree comes from an Aboriginal word 'Taree-bit' meaning 'fruit of the wild fig', a staple in the diet of my ancestors. According to my mother, I smiled up at her and dad on that first day without a worry in the world. They however had much to concern them.

Life on a mission was particularly difficult, especially for the men. The rules imposed by the Aborigines Welfare Board had a devastating effect on them. Aboriginal men were by nature the hunters and food providers, but mission life obliterated their role and their identities. Their hereditary ways weren't just discouraged. They were outlawed. If my Dad brought a kangaroo back to the mission to cook, he would be punished by a reduction in flour rations. If the kangaroo was shared with other families, their rations were also cut. Fishing was prohibited and done in

BACK ON THE BLOCK

Traditional life in the Purfleet region: fishing and hunting.

secret. Withholding the weevil-ridden flour ration was a regular punishment, but there was nothing else, as it was a staple food needed by all of the families. A kangaroo, rabbit or wallaby only ever supplemented the already scant rations allotted. Strangely, instead of the manager taking the view that our catch would just top up the food already supplied, he subtracted rations to keep everyone on minimum levels. Men on the mission felt constantly humiliated.

As children, we knew none of this. My world was not the world of stories around the campfire, of hearing Dreamtime tales of animals, spears and water holes. I knew nothing of our ancestors' skills in hunting and dot painting. Neither was it the world where children went off to school every day and had piano lessons and rode ponies. I was living in an in-between 'assimilated' world and I just got on with playing the games that kids play. After me, Mum gave birth to a baby boy whom they named Luke, but unfortunately he died soon after from diphtheria. Two and a half years later my brother Murray came into the world, then fifteen months later my brother David was born. Space was now getting short. The bed was getting crowded but there was one more sibling to come. My brother Lenny arrived when I was about seven years old, and my family was complete.

Sunday was the only bright spot in our dull mission week, when we were permitted to go to Uncle Berty Marr's church with other mission families. It wasn't the best church I've ever seen, but it was filled with people who cared about each other. We sang songs and listened with interest to what Uncle Berty had to say, and we always left in a better mood. Occasionally a fella named Mr Hermann used to come to church to play his piano accordion and tell stories to the kids. We enjoyed his visits. I had no way of knowing then, but he and I were to meet again much later in another place under very different circumstances. After church the children played out the back on an oval with a water well in the centre. Our parents warned us over and over again to stay away from it.

'Keep away from there or the Hairy Man will get ya after sundown and take ya away,' my parents warned. There would be plenty of Kooris out there who still remember the stories told to them about the 'Hairy Man'. It may be the same sort of threat that white kids heard about the Boogie Man. Once a young child went missing in the bush and we were told that the Hairy Man must have taken him. We never saw him again.

The dam behind our house wasn't just a source of food to us. We are from the Biripi people, a coastal tribe who have a close association with water, so the dam was the perfect place to spend time whenever we could. I couldn't have imagined life without it. Whenever a parent was looking for one of the children, the dam was the first place they'd check.

At Christmas time my Mum and Dad, along with my grandparents, aunts, uncles, cousins and friends, all left Purfleet to go down to a nearby beautiful coastal place called Saltwater, where we'd stay for six weeks from Christmas Eve. Even today this is a sacred part of the coast for the Biripi people, as it has been for many years.

This was the only time our people could reclaim some of the traditional lifestyle that was prohibited. Small details about how we used to live traditionally were passed on. I learned that our ancestors lived on seafood, possums, grubs and wild fruit. They made stringed musical instruments from wallaby tail sinew. I learned about the concept of recycling and thinking of others: that when eating fruits and wild bush food we did not put the seeds in a bin like whitefellas. We left them to be swept up by the river and transplanted somewhere else to grow for the next people to find them. Because of the relative isolation of Saltwater, the adults could talk about mission life away from outsiders.

The days we spent at Saltwater were a special time for us as children. We played and swam from daylight to dusk and ate our favourite food. The adults sat around singing and telling stories late into the night. Dropping off to sleep with those sounds in the background was very comforting. It gave me a sense of belonging, a sense of family and a feeling of being safe and secure, knowing that Dad and Mum were nearby. My father was strict about grog. There was no drinking in front of kids. Drinking wasn't a problem and those who wanted a drink did it away from the campsite. Most of my family were Christians and their beliefs sustained them more than any amount of grog could.

Our time at Saltwater always came to an end far too soon. The kids whined about going back but soon adjusted to mission life again. For reasons we didn't understand, the grown-ups were always sombre on their return to the mission, particularly the men. As soon as they returned from Saltwater they became withdrawn, sad and quiet. The cycle of humiliation had begun again. The women tried to make up for the men's sadness by being positive and keeping up the family's morale.

Down at the beach the men could escape the drudgery of mission life. With stories, songs and traditional food, Saltwater was like a release day from prison. Back at Purfleet there was nothing for them to do but miss the old ways. On rare occasions, permits to work outside the mission were granted, but most men spent their days sneaking off into the bush to play two-up and talk. Our times at Saltwater were carefree, full of laughter, but hanging over the good times was the realisation it wouldn't last. Every year going back was harder than the year before.

The more time passed, the more anxious my father became about living on a mission. He, like all others, longed for a different life for his family, an independent existence, away from the rules and regulations of a government-controlled community.

Purfleet Mission Hall and Residence, 1937.

Purfleet Mission schoolchildren with resident missionary Miss Maud Oldrey, 1910.

Purfleet Mission.

He could see that the mission system had not changed since he was a young man. The glaring reality was that any Aboriginal living on a mission would never be able to improve their lot. The low standards set by the authorities years earlier were still in use. Nothing had changed and nothing was about to change.

My father realised that he was going to have to leave Purfleet. He was never going to have a family life the way he dreamed of by staying where he was. He was tired of being controlled by the government, Boards, managers and by people who thought they knew best. He decided we had to move.

We had to sneak away when no-one was expecting it, such was the tight rein on the movements of Aboriginals within the mission system. Secrecy was most important, so we children weren't involved in any of the planning. One night in 1953, my parents woke their children, and under the cover of darkness, my family stole quietly out of Purfleet.

*

We went by train to Kendall. My granny Doris, along with Uncle Ray and Auntie Deb and their children, had already moved to Kendall, which made it easier for Mum and Dad to join them. Auntie Deb had told Dad about the shack next door to hers being vacant, so in we moved.

My parents were like new people in Kendall. They were much more at ease and far happier after the move from the mission. We settled into a little cottage, and Mum went about making our new place into a home. It was a little cramped, but in the Aboriginal culture family is everything, and it was better to be a little short of space than to have a homeless cousin or uncle. To my young mind, the more people there were, the more fun we could have.

My Mum slowed down that idea of having too much fun by enrolling me in the local school. I was more interested in exploring the bush and fishing holes than starting school, but school had its good side; it only went for six hours and we got to play at lunchtime. School in Kendall was held in the old picture theatre; it was small and not too strict. Science, music and art were my favourite subjects and I always tried to do my best in them. The best part about going to school was the sports, especially soccer, which was my favourite of all the field games.

Dad had become a changed man since moving to Kendall. Not long after we arrived there he started working for the local section of the Forestry Department. Unfortunately it wasn't full-time work and so he had to work as a boxer for the different shows around the district. He was a very fit, muscular man who was good at boxing and who had won quite a few fights on the show circuit. Together with his brothers and cousins, he trained in boxing with the famous Dave Sands. We missed him when he was away, but after a while we got used to his coming and goings. Life was best though, when he was working in the forests nearby.

I had a close cousin who went by the nickname Boxy. He and I spent a lot of time together looking for different ways to get some pocket money. We picked ferns for display windows and collected bottles for return money. If we had enough money we'd go to the local baker and buy bread. Then with the smell of it wafting in our nostrils we'd race back home, spread butter and Vegemite on it, and scoff it down while it was still warm. Often our Nan would take us down to the beach to help her collect shells. She would clean them up and use them to make craft, at which she was gifted, and then Boxy and I would sell them.

On the weekends the school reverted to a picture theatre. Our bottle collection money meant that sometimes we could see a film and eat lollies as well. There had been nothing like it back on the mission.

Every year Kendall had its local show and we always looked forward to it impatiently. Enough bottle collection money meant we could go on rides, eat hot dogs and go to Sideshow Alley. As soon as the show was over we'd go around the grounds again, looking for more bottles. We weren't the only ones doing it; there was a lot of competition around from the other kids.

Our other activities in Kendall included picking pears and persimmons and taking them home to Mum to make jams. I don't think I'll ever taste jam like that again in my life. It's a small thing I took for granted back then. Now, it has an important place in the memories that are left of my mother. We loved exploring the sawmill when it was closed on weekends, and going fishing. Occasionally a family friend, Mr Duck, would take us out in his boat where we fished from the middle of the river. Mum used to let us go further up the river than she normally would have because he was there keeping an eye on us.

Our wonderful new life at Kendall was to be short-lived. We were there about ten to twelve months when the government caught up with us. Mum and Dad had received a visit from the welfare people ordering us back to Purfleet. My Dad knew the authorities would be back, so he again planned an escape. I was almost seven years old then and was about to go to my third home. Going to the unknown was better than going back to Purfleet and back to rations handed out by the manager. Back to the sad faces and a hopeless future. Back to a life of total dependency. It was very likely they would impose some sort of punishment on us as well, because Dad and Mum had not been granted permission to leave the mission in the first place. These worries were far from the minds of children, but I'm sure my parents would have given it quite a lot of thought.

Ten days later my mother moved her children into Platts Estate, Platto we called it, in Newcastle. Our father had gone on ahead to arrange a house. The house was short on space and so the beds would be brought out at night and put away in the morning. It was at Platts Estate that my youngest brother Lenny was born. Room became scarce. When he was eight months old Lenny slept with me and my brothers, making bedtime a very crowded affair. There was one tap on the whole estate which everyone shared.

During this period my father worked locally for the state forests department. Many Aboriginals, including my father's cousin and his brothers, worked in this industry around Raymond Terrace and Bulahdelah and other places. Once when my father was fooling about with his brother Shane in the forest, Dad kept putting his little finger on the stump and said, 'Go on try and cut it off.' He pulled it away twice just in time, but on the third time, it happened. The final swing resulted in Uncle Shane cutting the end off Dad's finger. As it fell to the ground, Uncle Shane and Dad looked at each other in surprise, laughed, and carried on working as best they could.

Every year when the wet weather came, my father followed the shows until the forests were workable again. He was usually only gone for a couple of weeks at a time. When the show season wasn't running and rain prevented forestry work, he'd have to go out to collect bush tucker to feed us all. Bush tucker is good food but there wasn't much variety. Dad said we were too fussy. I suppose we were a bit spoilt, because usually his regular wage supplied most of our needs, except for the unnecessary extras that we were wanting.

Occasionally Dad took me chicken stealing with him. We never got caught doing this and we only did it when times were difficult. It wasn't the ideal way to feed a family but there were six mouths to feed. I never considered Dad dishonest; he was just doing what he had to do. When there was no money coming in we often ran out of other items as well, but it was just a case of making do until the work started again.

Generally life at Platto was good, and we spent a lot of nights playing under the only streetlight on the estate. When we played cowboys and Indians I used to like being a cowboy and the Indians used to always lose. It strikes me as ironic that even at that age the Indigenous people were on the losing end — only this time it was by other Indigenous kids in another country, just playing games.

We kids played soccer, baseball (with an ordinary carved stick), red rover, cricket, marbles and brandie. We made our own billy carts which we'd race, and we'd also use them to collect scrap metal for money. We'd slide down hills on sheets of iron and race each other. I also used to love carving toys out of clay.

Life at Platto turned out to be one of the happiest times of my life. With so many relatives around us, it was comforting going from house to house visiting everyone. I know I took it for granted at the time, but later on I realised just how lucky we were to have parents like ours.

The fact that my Dad was so well respected by the other Aboriginals around the estate made me very proud of him. He was a hard worker in the forest, the best boxer on the estate and a man of principle. He was strong too. He once carried me a mile and a half to hospital when I was injured, most of the walk uphill. And he was kind. If anyone needed a hand then our Dad would be there to offer his help.

It didn't happen often, but if a fight did start at home he'd stop it straight away. Dad was determined to keep us free from violence and aggressive behaviour. The other men all seemed to take notice of what he said. He went to Brisbane to fight in the preliminary bouts, back when Alf Wells fought in the world title fight. My father's success gave me strong feelings of comfort and pride. I idolised him for his talent as a boxer and his kindness as a father.

My father was an epileptic. I asked him only once about the fits he had and then instantly regretted the question. About thirty seconds after I had asked him, he had one, right in front of me. At first I thought he was just showing me what happens during an attack, but then I realised it was a genuine epileptic fit and I didn't know what to do. I ran and got Mum. She knew straight away what needed to be done to help him. I never mentioned the topic again.

When it came to his children, he, like all the other dads, insisted we obey him at all times. The other kids used to get into trouble a lot more than we did. My brothers and I had a wonderful father. He was firm, fair and never forgot to give us a hug when he was coming home or going away. I suppose Mum and Dad must have been fairly pleased with us boys, because we didn't really get into too much trouble. Well we didn't get caught too often anyhow. I grew up knowing he was a good man, but just like many other young sons, I didn't appreciate him enough.

As the children in our family grew older we began to be aware of the anxiety that our parents lived with concerning the authorities. The welfare people came into Platto about once every four to six weeks. Sometimes we'd see them sitting on a nearby hill with binoculars, spying, waiting for the right time to strike.

'Run and hide,' our parents shouted as soon as a car was spotted. They told us that if the welfare people found us, we'd be taken away.

'Why whitefellas wanna take us away?' I asked.

We weren't told the reason but like all children at Platto we knew what to do. Once, Boxy and I were running to hide from the welfare people and luckily there was a well near some trees, camouflaged by bushes. We could hear them up above, stamping and yelling in frustration. They didn't find any of us that day, but we knew they'd be back to try again. It was just a matter of time.

STOLEN

Taken away

They must have been very quiet. We hadn't heard anything at all: no sound of a car pulling up, no crunch of footsteps on the path. They had picked their time. It wasn't the first time they had come. Platts Estate often received unwelcome attention from the Aborigines Welfare Board. This time, however, they had planned it in advance, waiting until my father was away working. They had been watching the house.

It was winter 1957, seven o'clock in the morning. The sun was up and the sounds of birds drifted down into our small kitchen. My brother Lenny was sitting on the floor, eating toast; my brothers Murray and David and I, rubbing our eyes in a state of half sleep, were waiting for mum to smear Vegemite on our bread before we dressed for school. A routine day in the Simon household.

Someone rapped loudly on the door. My mother didn't answer it. We hadn't heard anyone come up the path. The knocking got louder, and finally my mother, who was reluctant to answer any callers when my father wasn't home, opened the door and exchanged words with three people. We strained to hear what they were saying. Three men then entered the room. A man in a suit ordered my mother to pick up Lenny and give him to me. My mother started to scream. One of the policemen bent down and picked up my brother and handed him to me. My mother screamed and sobbed hysterically but the men took no notice, and forced my brothers and me into a car. My mother ran out onto the road, fell on her knees and belted her fists into the bitumen as she screamed. We looked back as the car drove off to see her hammering her fists into the road, the tears streaming down her face. Then we saw her stand up, turn around and go back inside the house, shutting the door behind her.

In the back of the car my mind was racing. Why hadn't Dad been there to stop this? Why didn't Mum fight back? Why had she turned her back and walked inside? Why hadn't she told us to run and hide as we had been instructed to do when white men came? How could she have let this happen? Paralysing fear swept over me. I felt sick. Where were we going? Was this what had happened to the boy that went missing in the bush? Perhaps this man had come and taken him away too. Maybe the Hairy Man was true.

He wasn't the Hairy Man. His name was Mr Norris. He said nothing once we were inside the car. No explanation. No words to put our fears at bay. I knew the answers to my questions. Our mother did not want us any more. I was ten, it was the first taste of rejection, and it was by my own mother. It hurt. That three-second thought about my Mum not wanting us was to plague me for the next forty years.

Mr Norris took us to his house.

'You'll be staying the night,' he said. 'And don't misbehave.'

He said we would be staying at his house until the court case the following morning. Now panic flooded my body. What court case? Court cases were for people who did the wrong thing. What did we do wrong? The three of us older boys stood together not knowing what we were supposed to do next. Lenny must have been able to sense the distress, because he started screaming and no amount of cuddling and rocking comforted him. He wanted his mother. We all did.

'Don't worry,' I told my brothers. 'Dad 'n' Mum'll be comin' to get us.'

Mr Norris's wife seemed to be a friendly woman, but it was obvious right away that he overruled her. She looked to him for approval before coming over near me to take Lenny into her arms to calm him down. She tried her best but she wasn't his mother. He held his arms out to his brothers, crying loudly, and finally Mrs Norris passed him back to me.

It was fairly obvious that Mr Norris had no time for any of us. He told us to go out into the backyard and keep quiet. I wondered if he was actually enjoying what was happening to my brothers and me — it certainly felt like it.

At dinnertime we were told to sit down and eat the food placed before us. We just weren't hungry.

'You lot are bad and wasteful,' he said.

That didn't make us feel hungry. It made us more traumatised. Dinner over, he ordered us to our beds and his wife said a quiet goodnight to us. When we were under the covers we were told in a very stern voice to go to sleep and not to speak. I lay there terrified, not knowing whether to cry, or to yell out for Dad to come and get us. Lenny had cried himself to sleep, exhausted. Murray lay there staring up at the ceiling and David was sobbing, hard at first and then more gently until he finally fell into an uneasy sleep. My head whirled with the events of what was happening. Confusion and fear and anger mingled together, and it took a very long time before I went to sleep myself. I had dreams of being hit by Mr Norris, dreams of my mother turning her back.

A harsh voice broke into my dreams.

'Get up and get dressed,' it barked.

It was morning. But there were no bird calls, no warm kitchen, no smiling face preparing Vegemite on toast. We put our day-old clothes on and sat on the beds, staring at each other, not knowing what to say. We looked down at our feet, looked at each other and looked down at our feet again.

Norris's face was set in an early morning snarl as we entered the kitchen.

'Sit down and eat everything that is put in front of you,' he ordered.

It had been twenty-four hours since we had eaten and now we were hungry. After a quick bowl of cereal we were once again herded into the car.

'Are we bein' taken back home to Mum and Dad?' David whispered.

I looked at him and shook my head. Panic started to set in once again. Lenny, being only two, was content now that he had slept and been fed. The rest of us were sitting on the back seat with fear growling in our stomachs and tears in our eyes. Mr Norris finally pulled up at the Newcastle courthouse and after parking the car he told us to get out and to follow him.

We were bundled into a courtroom, and there, in front of the court, were Mum and Dad, looking dejected. A man in uniform and Mr Norris sat us over to one side of the room. A man came into the court from out the back and everyone stood up as he sat down. Men in the front row were standing up and talking, saying things to the magistrate. I couldn't understand what they were talking about. Nor could I understand what the magistrate was saying. I know now that the court was accusing my father of neglecting us because he was away when the welfare came. What wasn't mentioned was that Dad was only away when he was working, and he was working to feed his family.

My mother was crying, wiping her eyes. Dad stood with his hand on her shoulder, pointing over at us. Lenny was now starting to cry as well. David looked over at Mum and seeing her distress, he cried too. Murray stared at the floor, a frozen look on his face. I was close to tears and feeling totally bewildered and powerless.

After more conversations, which I did not understand, the magistrate waved his hand at us and declared the court session finished. It was then that Mum started crying out aloud. Mr Norris and another man stood up and came over to us. I looked at Mum and Dad, waiting for them to say something. At first they were silent. Mum was looking at Dad and he was shaking his head from side to side, saying, 'No! No!' Then he started to yell at the magistrate. I thought things would be all right now; Dad was shouting and when he raised his voice, people took notice. Not these people. A policeman came and stood beside him, saying something in his ear. Mr Norris put his hand heavily on Murray's shoulder. He told the three of us to get up and walk out the front of the courthouse and get into the back of his car. My father was shouting at the magistrate and my mother was weeping on his shoulder.

Once again we were in the car with Mr Norris. Once again, driving to a destination unknown. My parents were now standing on the path in front of the courthouse. They were looking up the road at us as the car sped away. David was crying and Murray and I were beside ourselves with fear that gnawed at the pits of our stomachs. I had just put Lenny onto the seat beside me when Mr Norris stopped up the top of Hunter Street outside a shop. He got out of the car and then put his head back in the window saying, 'Wait here, I'm just going to get some cigarettes, I won't be long, so just sit still.'

We had to move quickly. I picked up Lenny and then said to Murray, 'Grab David and run!' We got out of the car, ran around the corner and up the hill as fast as we could. There was a bus pulling up which had a sign saying 'Waratah' on its front.

The bus stopped and we boarded. The ticket collector asked for our fares. I pretended to look in my pockets.

'Lost all me money,' I told him. He smiled as he looked down at Lenny.

'Just this once,' he said.

We got off at the stop nearest to our Auntie Deb's place and told her our story. She looked anxious and said we needed to get away as fast as we could. She gave us some food and money for bus fare and told us to run and hide up in the bush until Mum and Dad came along.

We caught the bus that went to the edge of Platts Estate because I wanted to get some clean clothes for us all. By now the two youngest brothers were hungry, so I sent Murray down to the shop to buy some broken biscuits. You got more in the bag if you ask for the broken ones.

While we were waiting for Murray to come back with the biscuits, we sat down on the bench just as a blue Holden pulled up. Two policemen got out.

'G'day,' they said. 'What're your names and where you goin'?'

'I'm Billy,' I said. 'This is me brothers and we're on our way to see our Nan.'

With a smile one of them told us to jump in and they'd give us a ride down there. Not realising they would know anything about the court session, we accepted the offer. I was also relieved that I wouldn't have to carry Lenny as my arms were getting tired.

As soon as they turned the car around, I realised they had no intention of going to Nan's. Murray and I looked at each other despairingly as the car turned into Mr Norris's street and pulled up outside his house.

'Thanks, fellas,' said Mr Norris to the police. 'I can look after them now.'

He waited until the police car had disappeared and then he pulled out a large stockwhip and cracked it, shaking it at us.

'If yous run away again, you're gonna get this!'

Our parents had never hit us, so when we saw the whip poised to strike we were terrified. Mr Norris was really angry and he continued to berate us as he took the biscuits off Murray and pushed us inside the house. He shoved me so hard I wet my pants in fear. Later that day he gave us something to eat, telling us to empty our plates or else. After lunch he sent us into the room we had slept in previously and told us to stay there. I sat on the bed, trying to organise the thoughts that whirled around in my mind, and at the same time tried to reassure Murray and David that we'd be all right. Judging by the looks they were giving me I don't think I was too convincing.

A few hours later Mr Norris came to get us for dinner. He said we had to wash our hands and be quiet as we sat at the table. Mrs Norris was there at the table and she smiled and said hello. We ate our food in silence, and as soon as we finished the meal he sent us all to bed. That night we were more frightened than we had ever been before.

The next morning after breakfast it was back in the car. He didn't talk and neither did we. I didn't ask and he didn't say where we were going, but it must have been a long way as we were in the car for hours. We stared out the window at an unfamiliar landscape. There were cows in the paddocks eating green grass, sharp corners, steep hills, passing cars, and then suddenly we stopped in Taree. Mr Norris got out opened the back door. Lenny was sleeping on my lap. Waking up and seeing Mr Norris looking at him, he screamed in fright. He screamed even louder when Mr Norris picked him up and carried him into a building. Mr Norris was gone for about twenty minutes and then he was back again, only this time without Lenny. There was no explanation of the whereabouts of our brother and we were too afraid to ask. Fear settled in. We wondered what had happened to Lenny and what was going to happen to us.

Hours later we came to a place called Kinchela. It was nighttime. Mr Norris drove the car through the gates and pulled up in front of a building. He again told us to stay put, while he went and spoke to a man who was waiting nearby. Minutes went by but they seemed like hours. What was this place? Would our brother join us? Was this our new home? Questions banged inside our heads.

Finally, Mr Norris handed us over to the manager. His voice was hard, his eyes cruel. It was this man and others like him, who would change my mind about how I saw life, my family, my people, the white man and the morality of mankind in general.

Had I remained at home, I would have learnt many lessons from my father as I grew up. I would have found employment, had a girlfriend, and been given all the opportunities other boys had. My future was now in the hands of strangers, and even though I didn't know it at the time, they were purposely going to make my life miserable for a long time to come. These men were about to change what should have been a normal Aboriginal youth. Nothing would ever be the same again.

The new boys

The manager, Mr Borland, came out to the car, and he and Mr Norris shook hands as if they were long-lost friends. Our plight was totally ignored as they swapped pleasantries. Then Borland ordered us out of the car and into a building. This was the place that was to be our new home, and even though I had never heard of the Kinchela Boys' Home I was sure that I wouldn't like it one bit.

Mr Borland organised all the paperwork and then said that the first thing to be done was to check out our condition. He looked us up and down then asked us our names. I gave him mine first, and then, because of a deafening silence, I told him my brothers' names as I pointed to them. Mr Borland wrote them down on three cards and three pieces of paper. Each form had a number on the top of it and he told each of us what our number was and to make sure we remembered them. Mr Borland said first up we had to have a haircut and a shower. He pointed to a nearby door and motioned us to go through it.

P. O. Box 180,

KEMPSEY,

9th July 1957.

The Superintendent,
    Aborigines' Welfare,
    Sydney.

SUBJECT: William Simon, Born 30.3.'47, Martin Simon, born 22.10.'50, Desmond Simon, Born 14.1.'52, Lawrence Simon, born 13.8.'54, Half-caste, C. of E.

REFERENCE: My telephone conversation with the Superintendent on 3.7.'57.

    The abovenamed children were charged as Neglected Children and brought before the Children's Court at Newcastle on 8th July, 1957.

    They were committed to the care of the A.W.B.

    Lawrence Simon was admitted to St. Christopher's Children's Home (C. of E.), Taree on the 9th. Prior to being admitted to the Home, it was necessary for me to have him placed in the Taree Hospital for 48 hours for diphtheria and infectious diseases tests to be carried out.

    The Matron of the Home offered to collect the child from the hospital after 48 hours, and will forward his measurements for a clothing Outfit.

    The other three boys were committed to the Boys' Home at Kinchela on the same day.

    Please find attached a copy of my evidence given in Court. Committal papers pertaining to the case are big being posted to the department by the Court, as it was 4.45 p.m., when the case was finished, and there was no time to complete the necessary papers.

(Sgd.) A. NORTON,
Aborigines' Welfare Officer.

Letter to Aborigines' Welfare, July 1957

We quietly walked into the next room, where another man was waiting to cut our hair. In no time at all my hair was on the floor, after being roughly hacked off with blunt scissors. By the time the man had finished cutting we were almost bald. We were left with our heads covered with small cuts and grazes.

Next we were told to have a shower. We were told to remove our clothes and as soon as we did, they were taken away and thrown into a bin. Without a word an assistant poured disinfectant on each of us, then washed us all over. He was very rough and I formed the impression that he was deliberately trying to hurt us. Every place on our bodies was prodded, scrubbed and inspected.

We finished drying ourselves and then were sent into the medical room. There a man in a white coat looked into our ears, under our arms, around our groins and backsides, as well as into our mouths. We stood totally humiliated throughout the inspection. The man was quite rough, saying, 'Open wider, wider!' as he looked into my mouth. He made notes on his forms as the inspection went on. After he had finished checking the three of us over, he told Mr Borland that David had a minor ear infection which needed attention, but Murray and I were fine.

With the medical over we were each handed a pair of pyjamas with the number Mr Borland had given us earlier printed on the pocket, and a shirt and pair of shorts also. I was number thirty-three. Not Bill. Not even Simon. Just number thirty-three.

We were shown our dormitories, and Mr Pooley, the guard, explained the dorm rules. He then allocated beds to each of us.

'That's where you'll be sleeping from now on, and don't forget which bed is yours. You wet the bed, you'll have to wash your own sheets. And you'll be punished as well.'

We wouldn't be sleeping side by side. I would be away from my brothers, but the rules were that the boys slept in their age groups. The young ones aged five, six and seven were in the first section, and eight- and nine-year-olds were next, and then came the ten-, eleven- and twelve-year-olds up the other end. This meant David was up one end, Murray was in the middle and I was up the other end. Boys who had been troublesome were made to sleep on the beds right outside the guard's door.

I sat on my bed, looking around at all the other boys. There were about thirty of us. I can still see their faces in my mind today: the sad faces, the lack of expression, of spirit, of life. Each boy was looking from David, to Murray and then at me. No-one said a word to us; they obviously knew better.

During that first night at the Home I could hear my brothers sobbing for most of the night. They weren't the only ones. The boys who had arrived in the previous days were still getting upset at bedtime. It seemed to take a few weeks for each boy to settle down. Everyone coped differently, depending on their ages and their circumstances. My crying had to be done quietly, or else David would hear me and become even more unsettled. I lay there at night, knowing I couldn't do anything to help either of my brothers. I couldn't even be physically near them.

I wondered what had become of Lenny and whether we would ever see him again. Dad would be angry at me for not looking after him better than I had, because I was the eldest and Dad was always telling us to keep an eye on him whenever Mum wasn't near. I felt I had failed my father. The more I thought about it, the more I knew he'd be angry with me when he came to take us home. I felt hopeless about my own failure to protect my brother. I started crying softly, remembering that the others weren't allowed to hear me. It was long after most of the other boys were asleep before I finally drifted off some time in the early hours of the morning. I believe that first night was the saddest and loneliest I have ever been in my life. I stayed awake most of the night, hoping our parents would come and get us. They never came. No-one came. I hoped that they would come in the next few weeks. Even when those days turned into weeks and the weeks turned into months I still didn't give up hope.

The first night was always the hardest for any new boy at Kinchela. I saw it year after year. Scared young boys were being held for no apparent reason in a strange place against their will and with absolutely no compassion from their captors. It was a true recipe for sadness and misery. For as long as we were at Kinchela, we never really stopped being scared. The guards seemed to take great delight in making sure that we remained frightened and insecure at all times.

At six o'clock in the morning we were told to have a shower, then wash and comb what was left of our hair. Fingernails and hands had to be cleaned thoroughly. We would be punished if they were dirty. After we showered we stood in front of our beds and one of the guards came down and checked to see if anyone had wet the bed. Once he'd done that, he yelled for us to get outside and line up. Being new we didn't really know what to do or where to go, so my brothers followed me and I followed another boy about my age. After a couple of days we got to know the routine and more importantly, learnt what we needed to do to avoid being punished. Unfortunately for us that was easier said than done.

Kinchela had a system of trustees, older boys whose job it was to allocate chores to us and make sure we didn't misbehave. Not one of them was friendly. In fact, they made us feel frightened. Each day there were jobs to be done before parade and before we went to school. Age determined what job we were given. Young ones had to sweep the paths, polish the copper doorknobs, wash the lower windows and other small tasks.

My first job, accompanied by two others my age, was to sweep the paths around the buildings every morning. We were given brooms and the trustee pointed out where we were to sweep. Mr Borland inspected everything as he walked around to make sure all was clean and tidy. David and Murray were given rags to polish the doorknobs.

We hadn't been issued with any shoes to wear and our feet were frozen on the cold grass and cement. I looked at the other two boys I was with and saw that their feet were badly cracked and obviously very sore. They didn't say anything to the trustees about their wounds though, because they knew the consequences of complaining. On that first morning I noticed that every single boy was barefooted. No-one wore shoes around the grounds. The boys who worked in the dairy wore gumboots while they did the milking, but as soon as they were finished they too had to remain barefooted unless they were attending high school. None of the children under twelve ever wore shoes or boots, even in winter. Everyone had sore feet.

Class at Kinchela Boys Home.

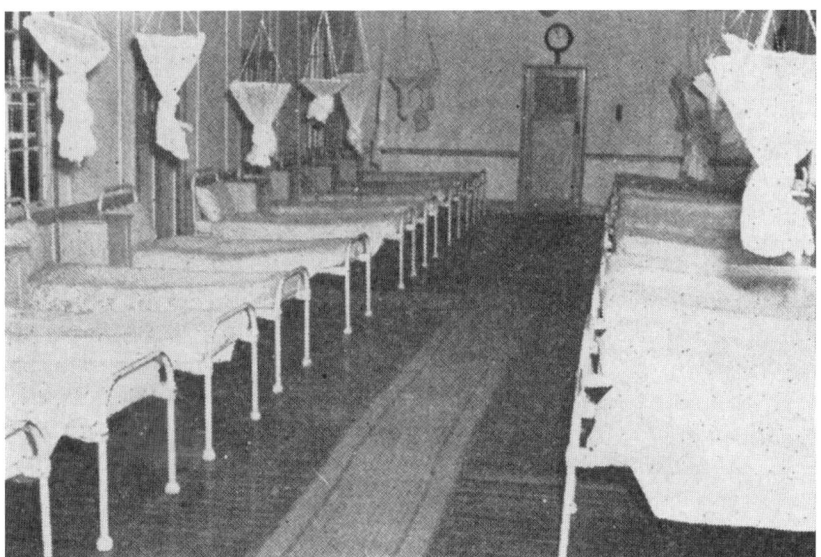
A dormitory at Kinchela.

It cannot be over emphasised that these boys at Kinchela are not delinquents. They have been committed to the Home by Order of the Court, because they have hitherto been neglected or have become orphaned, or at the request of their parents.

— *Dawn*, March 1952

This drawing by Albert Cooper, 12, is typical of his work and shows great talent. Albert's schoolteacher is very impressed by his work, and Mr Henricksen is encouraging Albert in his drawing and painting

IT'S ALMOST LIKE A COUNTRY CLUB AT KINCHELA

Koala drawn by Albert Cooper, aged twelve, resident in Kinchela in 1965.

When I first became a work boy and had to milk the cows, we were not issued with gum boots straightaway. In the middle of winter our feet froze till they ached and so we kept them warm by standing in fresh, steaming cow excrement. Often it was a race, a matter of which cow excreted first and who got there first to stand in it and warm up.

At exactly eight o'clock every morning we had to line up on parade. It was here that we first met the guard named Mr Seaton. The guards at Kinchela were all ex-army personnel. The manager was a former captain and one staff member had been a sergeant in the Grenadiers. Two guards were standing beside Mr Borland, who was about to go through the names of the boys who would not be getting any breakfast. They were being punished for wetting their beds the previous night.

Six boys' names were called out. They lined up to be caned and after they had been hit twice on the hands, they stood back in line, crying. With the punishment over, the rest went off to have their breakfast, while the six boys had to go wash their bedclothes and sheets and then hang them on the line to dry. For the young boys under ten years old, bed-wetting was usually their worst infringement of the rules. On any given night about six to eight kids wet the bed. It was usually the most recent inmates who did this. No connection was made by the authorities between the trauma of having being taken and bed-wetting. It was a simple matter of being troublesome.

My brothers were still crying in their beds at night. No matter how much I tried to put them at ease during the day, soon after they went to bed, they would start to cry. I could always tell when Murray or David was crying even amongst the others that were doing the same. The sound of my brothers sobbing pierced my heart, but there was nothing I could do but lie in my bed at the other end of the dormitory. I knew that if I went to comfort them, I would be punished. I had to wait until the guards were in their quarters at the far end of the dormitory before I would quietly crawl along the floor to my brothers' beds. Staying crouched down I would talk softly with them.

'Shh...Mum and Dad'll be comin' to get us. Stop cryin' or I'll get caught outa bed.'

Sometimes this would quieten them down, but there were times when I just couldn't calm them and eventually I'd have to go back to my bed and leave them to cry themselves to sleep. Leaving your bed after lights out was punishable by caning at the next parade. The youngest boys cried the most and once one had started, others would soon follow. The younger they were the longer it took them to get used to their new life.

The new, harsh and uncaring lifestyle made sure that David and I continued to wet our beds for the next two years. None of us had wet the bed when we had lived with our parents but we more than made up for it when the problem started at Kinchela. Being beaten and yelled at so often caused us to be continually anxious. It wasn't always a result of us being punished either. Seeing other boys being belted and punched was just as frightening, especially if it was happening to your brother or a friend. Because we were scared we wet the bed. Because we wet the bed we were punished, and being punished made sure we remained scared, thus causing us to wet the bed again. There was no escape from this vicious cycle.

Something had to be done to stop the beatings we were receiving for wetting our beds. Eventually I taught myself to wake up as soon as I had wet my bed. Once awake I'd crawl along the floor to David's bed and check his sheet to see if it was dry. It was always wet so I would quietly pull the sheet off his bed and remove his pyjama pants as well. I'd crawl back to my bed, grab my sheet, wrap up the bundle and creep into the boiler room. Once there, I'd wash everything to the best of my ability, then stand and dry them near the boiler, all the while hoping I wouldn't be caught. As soon as everything was dry, I'd go back and place David's sheet back under him and put his pyjama pants back on. Then I'd go back to my bed, put my sheet on and get up at the normal time, as if nothing had happened.

Come morning, check-up time, the guards wouldn't even know we'd wet our beds. As long as neither of us wet the sheet a second time before the morning wake-up call, we'd be all right. Unfortunately, if David's bed was dry when I checked it but wet before morning, then it was impossible to help him. The guard would check the bed, and after finding it wet David would be brought out onto morning parade and punished. Then he'd be forced to wash his bedding by hand while the others were having breakfast. Usually I was able to help him to do his washing and slip him a bit of food that someone else had saved for him.

It took about a month before any of the other boys would start talking and being friendlier towards newcomers. There were some who couldn't speak very good English but eventually they found their place in a group. Some took longer than others. It took me just on two years to really settle in properly. There were cultural differences between the boys and also cultural similarities, but the guards discouraged bonding with one another and would tell untruths in order to create disharmony. The government policy of the day was that brothers and sisters from the same family were taken, but only one family per area was taken, so that ties with any other friends in the community were severed. Similarly, when a boy turned eighteen he was often sent out to work, but he was purposely never returned to the area from which he had come. This ensured that family ties which had been lost were not renewed.

All meals at Kinchela were preceded by a roll call with a guard yelling out your number, to which you replied, 'Here sir.' Nothing else was acceptable. As time went on, we all knew everyone else's number, so if we heard a number being called to go to the office, we knew who it was straight away. All of our clothes were marked with our numbers on them. This number was a very important tool used by the authorities to make sure we took on as little personality as possible. We all wore exactly the same style of clothing: grey shorts and grey short-sleeved shirts, and we wore them everywhere we went. They were styled in such a way that people could tell without doubt that we were from the Kinchela Boys' Home. Whenever we were out in public, everyone knew who we were. The last thing Kinchela wanted was for any of us to strike up friendships with anyone outside the Home.

At nine o'clock in the morning, after parade, Monday to Friday, all kids under twelve had to go to the school building in the compound. It wasn't far from our dormitory to the schoolroom. Our teacher was Mr Telfour and he was very different to the guards. As it happened our teacher was a good ally for us, because occasionally the manager or one of the guards would walk into the classroom and look about, but they would never say anything to us while Mr Telfour was there. The subjects we studied were the same ones we had studied at Waratah, and thankfully we weren't given homework. Mr Telfour always called us by our names and not our numbers. When we made mistakes with our schoolwork, he would always show us how to do it properly. I don't remember Mr Telfour ever punishing us for getting something wrong or for misbehaving. I had the impression he knew we were belted enough already. He was the only decent man in the whole place, but he was only there from nine in the morning until three thirty.

No boy was issued with shoes until he went to high school. The only time they let us wear shoes was to the high school in Kempsey. The boys would put them on before school, then be made to take them off as soon as they returned to the Home. The boys who went to Kempsey High wore a grey shirt and long trousers and were also issued with a red-and-blue-striped school jumper. When they returned from school, they took off their grey school clothes and put on their grey Home clothes. Everyone from the Home loved going to high school as it was an opportunity to get away for a while.

Once the boys turned fifteen they were known as 'work boys'. They now did harder, more manual jobs such as the outside farm work. This involved ploughing fields, planting crops, digging the silage pits, working in the dairy, milking the cows, general maintenance, cutting grass and baling it and maintaining the fences. As well as the outside chores they were involved in the practical daily running of the Home: the kitchen duties, which included helping the cook prepare the meals for the boys and the staff, setting and clearing the tables, washing dishes, mopping floors and serving the meals. The bonus for those working in the kitchen was that they could often siphon off the best food for themselves.

Cleaning was often a point of contention because it was hard to satisfy the guards' standard of cleanliness. Work boys also did other general domestic work like cleaning the dormitories, cleaning the toilets and the bathrooms, and sweeping and tidying the classrooms. It was continuous work, and by the end of the day bed was a welcome sight.

A roster system ensured that all boys knew which jobs they were allotted and when to do them. The roster was operated on a monthly basis. If you didn't do your job to the guards' satisfaction or when you were rostered to do it, punishment was harsh. It was better to continue working even when ill. If you reported sick the guards would straight away think you were loafing, and they'd be angry, taking their anger out on everyone else. Whenever we were sick we kept working, and the others would cover for us so that the guards wouldn't be suspicious.

At times I'd convince myself that eventually our Dad would come and take us home, back to the people who cared about us. I imagined playing with my cousins up the back of Platto. They were good thoughts to hold onto, but as time passed the chances of being reunited with our family were becoming smaller and smaller. The dream faded as the months passed.

So began my eight years at Kinchela, from the age of ten to eighteen. Here we were incarcerated and reprogrammed as part of what was known as the 'assimilation program', until we reached the age of eighteen, or until the Aboriginal Welfare Board found a place of work for us. We were not aware of the long legacy of policies that broke families apart, policies that stretched back from the Aboriginal Protection Board set up in 1883 to the Aborigines Welfare Board set up in 1940, all policies that had nothing to do with protection or welfare in any sense of the words. We were not there because we had no homes or no parents. We were not orphans, or neglected, or abused. We were not there because the government wanted us to have a better education. We were there simply because we were black.

Punishment

Punishment parade started at four o'clock each afternoon, and as luck would have it the high school bus would return us to Kinchela just in time for it. Mr Borland would be waiting eagerly, greedy for the voyeuristic pleasure of watching the physical punishment that was about to be meted out. Regardless of age, it was bare buttocks and two to six savage hits with a four-foot cane for those judged to have broken the rules. Caning was the preferred method of punishment for such crimes as speaking back to a white person in authority, wetting the bed, or not having clean hands or fingernails at inspection time. Whether you were guilty or not was not up for discussion. If you were called out on parade, in the minds of the guards you had broken the rules.

Minor infractions of rules were met with a boy being sent to bed early without any dinner, accompanied by a slap around the ears. Quite often if the younger boys missed out on a meal due to punishment, the older boys would hide food and give it to the young boys later.

Before each meal a cleanliness inspection took place. If your hands and face were not clean and tidy, you were made to stand out on parade and so missed out on your rations. There was always at least one boy who missed a meal each day. If we were unlucky we missed two rations in a day, but we tried hard not to let that happen. The dining room never had every boy present at any given mealtime. On average there would be at least three, possibly four boys missing.

Missing meals, however, was a mere inconvenience when compared with punishment parade. Any boy who had been reported to Mr Borland during the day for any wrongdoing (true or manufactured) would be called on to step forward. Sometimes we knew we'd be getting the cane at four o'clock, but quite often we had no idea until our names were called out. Then stomach muscles would tighten and hearts would start to pound. We'd look around at the others, trying to figure out what we were guilty of this time.

It was humiliating enough to have your name called out in front of other boys, but having to pull your pants down and expose your buttocks was far worse. Mr Borland would apply the strokes across our buttocks in such a way as to force the cane to wrap around our legs. The tip of it would land on the inside of the leg near our groins. Embarrassment was soon forgotten and replaced by an unbearable pain. Welts appeared quickly around our inner legs followed by multiple green and red bruises, which took days to heal.

Boys who spent time at Kinchela and received this sort of punishment remembered it long into their adult lives. I've spoken to many Kinchela boys over the years, and not one has said he was free of physical punishment during his time there.

Boys will be boys, and naturally there were occasions when we broke the rules, even deliberately, but far too often we would be caned for doing virtually anything the guards disagreed with or disliked. Mr Pooley in particular could be quite vicious. If he took a dislike to a certain boy then that boy would be reported on some made-up infringement. And more often than not the punishment was out of proportion to the crime.

The younger ones were in a most difficult position; because of their age and inexperience, they often broke house rules throughout the day and were totally unaware of it, acting on impulse. Quite often there were those who didn't even know all the rules, let alone abide by them. But that didn't prompt the guards or Mr Borland to exercise any leniency. From the first day all boys were expected to know all the rules and procedures then behave accordingly. The guards would see a very young boy do something wrong during the day and would then pass a report on to Mr Borland, usually embellishing a little in the retelling. The young boy would only find out about it at punishment parade.

We learnt quickly not to ask why we were being hit, because when we did ask, we received another stroke for our impertinence. You could see the bewilderment on the faces of the youngest as their names were called out. At six or seven years of age the punishment received at four o'clock was quite often a mystery, as we just didn't think to connect it to an incident that had been dealt with hours earlier by a guard.

The punishment parade wasn't the end of the ordeal. If Mr Borland decided to segregate a boy after caning, that boy would be taken away to the small punishment room.

During my time there, the sports equipment room doubled as the solitary confinement room. There was more pain and blood in there than there was sports equipment on any given day. A boy would usually be sent there for one to three days, depending on his infringement and the severity of his wounds. Whilst in solitary, he'd receive basic food and water only. It was thought that this time in confinement would improve our manners, but the real reason was to keep the boy out of sight until his lacerations healed to an acceptable level. On many occasions when on kitchen duty, I was the one responsible for passing the 'meal' to the boy being held in that room.

Words of comfort for the bleeding boy behind the door were usually not much comfort. Time spent in that room was always associated with pain and loneliness and nothing anyone said could help. A few of the work boys were often very angry and sometimes violent when they were locked up in there. When it was their mealtime, I'd place the food under the door and just leave it. It was no use trying to calm a boy who was in pain because of his wounds and who was also enraged at the punishment — and at times, possibly innocent of wrongdoing.

The punishment room was a small, dark, hot room with a tiny window high up, which did not open. Cricket bats and balls were piled in the corner close to the door, which had a gap of about six centimetres above the ground, just enough to pass a plate through.

Whenever the welfare inspectors came to the Home, the room suddenly reverted to a sports storage room. I used to wonder what would have happened had the authorities known about that sad, dark, hot little place of agony, punishment and grief and whether they would have done anything about it.

The high school boys had the unenviable position of being punished both at school and at the Home. Punishment at school was either in the form of lunchtime detention or a caning. Two to six lashes across the hands were the norm. The school used a thinner cane than Mr Borland used at the Home, but it still caused much pain. The difference between punishment at school and at the Home was that at school we were only punished if we really had done something wrong.

After punishment had been carried out, the Headmaster, no doubt thinking he was doing the correct thing, would then contact the manager at the Home to make a report about the wrongdoing and the punishment that had been administered. However on returning to the Home you would be called out to the front at the four o'clock punishment parade to be caned again, only this time with a much thicker cane.

I have always hoped that the school headmaster had no idea that we were being punished twice for the same thing.

By far the worst punishment Kinchela inflicted on its inmates was a barbaric practice called 'Walkin' down the line'. For many years it was adopted as their punishment of choice, but fortunately for my brothers and me they stopped it about a year after we arrived. There were stories of even the young boys receiving it, but I don't ever remember seeing anyone younger than twelve being sent 'down the line'.

This punishment involved all the boys; we were lined up from the youngest to the oldest. Mr Borland would call the name of the offender to come and stand between him and a work boy at the beginning of the line, in front of the youngest person. It was the work boy's job to be the 'striker'. The offender would stand in front of the first boy in the line and be punched by that boy. After a punch was delivered the offender would move on to the next boy, and it would be his turn to have a hit. Then on to the next boy and so on all the way down the line.

If Mr Borland didn't think a punch or a hit was hard enough, then that person would have to hit the offender again, only it had to be harder than his first punch. If Mr Borland still wasn't satisfied, he would call on the 'striker' to give the offender a punch. And this time he would definitely be struck as hard as Mr Borland required. So if you didn't hit the offender hard enough when it was your turn, you were actually making it worse for him, because he received your not-so-hard punch as well as the hard one from the striker. Even if the offender was a brother or a friend, that initial punch had to be hard enough to be deemed adequate so as to spare the offending boy even more pain. Mr Pooley taught boxing to the high school boys and the work boys, so they knew only too well how to deliver an effective punch.

Many boys had brothers in the Home, and having to inflict pain upon a member of your own family brought much grief. Mr Borland took special notice when a boy stood in front of his brothers, making sure the punches were being delivered with force. It wasn't natural for brother to hit brother, cousin to hit cousin, friend to hit friend. And all of us felt the injustice of having to be directly involved in someone else's punishment. An enormous feeling of inadequacy and shame was present among the older brothers because they felt they had failed to protect their siblings.

On one occasion a boy was walking down the line with cuts and bruises all over his face, arms and body. His brothers were in the line, crying out aloud and barely able to hit him as he passed by them. Blood flowed freely from wounds to his head and lips, his eyes severely swollen. About two-thirds of the way down the line his walk had became a stagger, but he knew better than to lay down before he reached the end. His brothers waved their arms in the air, screaming out for the other boys to stop hitting their brother so hard. The other boys had their heads down and some even had tears in their eyes as they delivered powerful punches to the already battered body of their helpless friend. Finally the boy reached the end of the line, quietly whimpering as blood from his face dripped onto the ground. Standing hunched over trying to relieve the chest and stomach pains shooting through him, he started to cry loudly. As Mr Borland walked back towards his office he yelled back at two of the older boys to put the boy in the 'sports room'.

The punches at the start of the line didn't hurt much as the first hitters were the small boys. But as an offender went further along the line the boys steadily got older and stronger and their punches were harder and gradually more painful. By the time the end of the line was reached the boy was always in great pain.

Extensive bruising from the waist up with patches of blue and green became apparent in a short time. Broken ribs left untreated were common occurrences, with shoulders and arms bruised and skinned bare. The upper and lower lips were left cut, swollen and bleeding. The eyes were left bleeding and puffed up. Their shape changed, making a boy's face look totally different. Vision would be almost nil and blood would flow freely from the mouth, nose and sometimes from the ears as well. Some would reach the end of the line crying quietly, while others would be yelling out in pain. There were those who screamed uncontrollably in pain, angered by their humiliating experience.

After the punishment the offending boy would be taken away and locked up in the sports room. More often than not he'd be unable to stand and would have to be dragged away. His only form of assistance was the wet rag thrown at him to clean himself up. Wounds were left untreated. During his three days in there his food would be passed under the door and no-one was allowed to go anywhere near him. This inhumane treatment affected the boys differently. Many of the older boys became aggressive, kicking at the door and yelling at anyone who went near them.

In the time I was at the Home, I was involved in six of these 'Walkin' down the Line' incidents. Fortunately for me, I was never the one who actually received the punches, but I was forced to do the punching and to see the results of those who were on the receiving end. This sadistic form of punishment was always accompanied by comments from the guards to make sure we were kept in our place, physically and psychologically.

'It'll teach you manners,' they said. 'You're garbage, animals... lower forms of life who deserve all you get.'

Part of reprogramming was to be told daily that black people were no good and we should have nothing to do with them, or each other for that matter. With this information battered into our heads, there was on occasions animosity between each of us as we got older. Not a lot, but enough so that some boys hated both black and white by the time they were sixteen or seventeen.

Each guard had a particular form of punishment that was their trademark. Mr Pooley and Mr Byrd would come up from behind, cup their hand and hit directly over the ear. Then their hand would slide up over the head, in a rubbing motion. This action left us feeling off balance and our ears would buzz for an hour or so. Often we had to hold back the urge to vomit, because if we did it would bring more vocal and physical punishment. This treatment was a very effective way of damaging the eardrum. Five-, six- and seven-year-olds were not exempt from this form of punishment, which caused long-term harm to our hearing.

Today there are many Kinchela boys with damaged ears. There are also medical reports in the government archives, 'explaining' how the ear damage occurred. 'X fell over and hurt his ear,' or 'X had developed an ear infection due to a cold, or from fighting with another boy.' There is no mention in the archives about hearing loss, vomiting, nausea, dizzy spells and headaches caused by blows from the guards.

Another of the guards had a habit of striking up a conversation with an inmate, deliberately bringing up topics that would make a boy angry. It was compulsory to reply to all of his questions and be respectful at all times. He would sometimes make mention of the fact that the boy hadn't had any visitors since his arrival at the Home.

'Your relations mustn't love you and they don't want you' or 'Your parents didn't care about you,' he would say.

Many boys became emotional when hearing this. They started to speak back, their voices becoming loud and insistent.

'Our Mum and Dad will come and get us and take us away from here.'

That would be enough for him to say, 'Are you being cheeky, you little black mongrel?' or 'Are you being rude, you little black bastard?'

Despite our protestations, he neither listened nor cared and would hit us hard across the ear or put us on the punishment report or both. At four in the afternoon, we would pay for those comments.

For some reason it seemed the colour of our skin was a measure of how badly we were treated. There were some boys at the Home who were removed from the Pilliga Scrub Mission, between Narrabri and Coonabarabran, and there was also another couple who were brought in from near Bourke in far western New South Wales. These boys were lank in body and very, very dark in colour. During their stay at Kinchela, this rich skin colour proved to be unfortunate for all of them. The darker you were, the more likely, the more often and the more severely you were punished. The darker-skinned boys were always getting into trouble for the most trivial of things, things that the rest of us would not necessarily have even been punished for. We all felt desperately sorry for them. They were in fact better behaved than a lot of the other boys, but still they were beaten, often and viciously. The Darby brothers, Daniel and Joel from the Pilliga Scrub, coped very well with the results of their beltings. One day Daniel Darby was in trouble for something that wasn't too serious; however when the punishment was meted out to him, it was far, far harsher than other less-dark boys received for the same infraction.

'How do youse put up with hidings like that?' Daniel was asked.

'It's awright, we used ta this now,' was the reply.

'You can't be used to this sort of treatment. I bet youse didn't get hit like that when youse were on the mission?'

Young Daniel replied, 'No, never did, but things different now, it's okay.'

'How much more of this can youse take?'

Daniel smiled. He was only thirteen, in enormous pain and he still managed a smile. The Pilliga boys were always smiling. We just couldn't understand how they did it. No matter what time of the day you saw them, they would be smiling at something, and sometimes even at nothing. It was as if they were oblivious to their surroundings and to the situations they were enduring. The other boys formed the impression that the blacker you were, the more you smiled.

We had a lot of respect for the Darby boys and it was partly due to the fact that the guards could never break them, no matter how cruel the punishment. We once overheard a conversation between two guards after one of the Darby boys had had a beating.

'You can't hurt those bloody Darby boys, ya just can't hurt 'em. They keep grinning at you and ya just gotta try to knock that smile off their black faces.' The first guard shook his head, bewildered.

'You'll just have to try a bit harder to get rid of their bloody stupid grins, won't you?' the other guard smirked, and then he said, 'For the life of me I can't understand those fellas either, but I admire them for their courage.'

Although we were glad we weren't as black as the Darby boys, we liked them immensely. As far as their behaviour and attitude went, we couldn't seem to fault them. We felt good being around them; they had a natural ability to lift our spirits and keep us in a good mood. Because the hidings and beatings they received never seem to bother them, I used to wonder if their smiles were a separate physical entity and not connected to their emotions. Now, I realise it was probably their way of coping, although it didn't always prove successful. I learned much later that two of those boys had hung themselves.

We tried to look out for the boys who were disabled. Ed had had polio when a small boy and as a consequence he was left with short bowed legs. Pete, who'd also had polio, mixed with everyone, although he was older than us. He was friendly and courageous and we admired him. Patrick was deaf and mute. Occasionally we'd swear at him and he'd smile back, but we all kept an eye on him. He could never hear when the bell went so we'd tell him using the sign language he had taught us.

One day, a new boy arrived, the younger brother of one of the older boys. Our new inmate, Henry, stood out from the start. Not only was he in a wheelchair as a result of polio, but he was dressed as a girl. I found out that he had been sent to the Cootamundra Girls' Home to be looked after because there were no other facilities that could care for him in his condition. Because it was a girls' home, they dressed him like a girl until he was sent to Kinchela.

If we thought that sleep was a welcome relief from the daytime terror, we would be proved wrong. There were random roll calls, at any time of the day or night. At midnight or two o'clock we were often woken up and told to stand at the head of our beds. The guard would call out our number and we had to answer, 'Here Sir.' If all were present we could return to our beds, but if someone failed to answer then all hell would break loose. The guard would call the number again. If there was still no answer he continued to call the rest of the roll. After the roll call was completed, we'd have to remain standing to attention at the end of our beds. The guard would then get the trustees to check the toilets and the immediate areas around the dormitory. If there was still no sign of the missing boy, the manager would be informed and he would come to the dormitory and ask all of us individually if we had seen anyone leave the dormitory.

I think Mr Borland knew we wouldn't say anything, even if we did know where the missing boy had gone. After we had answered 'No, sir,' we were required to remain at attention for a few hours, the guards hoping that someone would change their mind and divulge information. The manager would inform the police that one of the boys had gone missing. Eventually we would be dismissed and they would let us go back to our beds.

If the missing boy or boys weren't found in the immediate area, we never saw them again. A week or two later Mr Borland would always make a point of telling us that the missing boy had been caught. He said that the boy was in a lot of trouble and had been taken to jail or some other place of misery. Then he'd warn us not to be as stupid as the escaped boy had been, because the same thing would happen to us if we walked off. Of course we didn't know how true these stories were.

For some boys, the thought of bedtime brought more terror than any punishment that could be meted out during the day. Years later I learned that many boys had been sexually abused at Kinchela. I have heard stories from others that were there, particularly before my time, when conditions were even more brutal. I was spared this form of abuse but many were not. Later I also heard that boys turned on other boys. No one during my time would have been able to discuss this even it had happened. It would have been too shameful and we would have received a beating for talking about it. No one would have believed us anyway.

*

From about the age of twelve, I acquired a need to be popular with the other boys. They usually got a laugh out of the little pranks I'd play on them which in turn made me well liked with the other boys in the dormitory, both young and old.

On one occasion after the evening meal I stole a big fish head from the kitchen. After poking out its eyes and threading a piece of string through the sockets, I tied the big wet fish head onto my face. I completed the costume with a piece of sack bag from the dairy over my shoulders and wrapping a blanket around my body. After dark I crept over to the small boys' dormitory and furtively tapped on the window. It was past curfew but a few of the boys inside were curious enough to want to see who was out there at that hour. When their faces were close to the window I suddenly jumped up. They screamed in fright as I ran away. I hid my costume under the building then quickly slipped back into the dormitory and went to bed. I performed this prank about three times in two weeks, with the same amount of success each time.

Occasionally Mr Borland patrolled the grounds, accompanied by his two big Alsatians. Quite often he included a tour of the dorms and we had no way of knowing which nights he would be coming around. I imagine it was a good way of keeping an eye on the staff as well. One night about fifteen minutes after lights out, I decided to put on my fish head outfit, which was by now getting smelly. On my way over towards the small boys' dormitory, I heard a noise down in the bushes. I assumed it was a boy on his way back from the toilets so I crept along the hedge and then jumped out from behind it yelling loudly.

Unfortunately it was the manager and his two dogs. Everything happened at once. I yelled out again only this time it was in fright and the dogs both started barking. Mr Borland held on to them as tightly as he could, stamping his foot and yelling at them to stop barking and for me to stop running. Frightened and already thinking of the repercussions, I kept running, throwing the fish head onto the ground and letting the blanket fall. Mr Borland must have been just as surprised as I was, because he didn't try to set the dogs on to me. I ran back to my dormitory and jumped into bed pretending to be asleep, out of breath and terrified.

In the next minute all the lights came on. Mr Borland stood there, waving his arms and yelling at everyone to get out of bed and stand in line. He still had the dogs by his side and they were barking as loudly as he was yelling. His face was red with anger, and the more he yelled the redder his face seemed to get. The guards came out of their room at the end of the dormitory. We stood in line for a long time before the manager was calm enough to continue. The guards were looking at each other and at Mr Borland, waiting for information.

A dreadful silence enveloped the room. Mr Borland started walking along the line of boys, looking for the culprit. As he slowly passed each one he said 'No!...no!...not you!...no!...no!...', then he stopped in front of me.

'Thirty-three, I should have known it would be you!'

He ordered Pooley to fetch a cane. By now he was rocking from foot to foot in anger. The longer he waited for the cane to arrive, the quicker he rocked from foot to foot, all the while staring at me and squinting. Both hands were rolled into fists and his arms were bent at the elbows and shaking uncontrollably.

After what seemed like hours he was handed the cane. He ordered me to pull down my pants and bend over. I barely had time to bend over before he started hitting me. The strokes were very hard, fast and vicious. He hit me six or seven times, maybe more. He was out of control. The welts ran from my lower back to below my buttocks. The pain he inflicted that night was the worst I had felt since arriving at the Home. As he hit me he shouted, ordering me to follow his rules or I would get more of the same. There was a rhythm to his beating: one stroke per word. As soon as he had finished he thrust the cane back into Pooley's hand and without a word to anyone, left the dormitory.

Pooley ordered us back into our beds. I was so sore and stiff that getting into bed was difficult. Lying on my stomach, I was left to sob to myself as the searing pain burned into my legs and buttocks. I lay awake on the bed for hours and as the pain steadied down to a burning, throbbing ache, I started to wonder how he knew it was me. It was only as I turned over that I realised I had forgotten to remove the piece of sack bag from my shoulders when I dumped the blanket and fish head. I was caned quite a few times during my years at Kinchela, but that night was one of the worst. My pranks came to an end for a while.

Months later I went down to the boiler room, picked up some coal dust off the floor and rubbed it all over my face. I played the same trick as I had with the fish head and managed to get away with it four times. The last time I performed this trick Mr Borland happened to be in the small boys' dormitory.

Once again we were lined up but this time the manager walked past the other boys quickly and halted opposite me and without asking whether or not I was the guilty one, he ordered me to pull down my pyjamas bottom and turn around.

By this time baring our backsides in front of everyone was not as shameful as it once was, but this time he hit me so viciously I started to cry. It was as though he was putting an extra effort into it, because I could feel the ridges on my backside come up straight away. After he finished I stood there sobbing, unable to understand how he knew it was me, but all became clear very soon. As he was leaving he turned and said, 'Now go and wash that black stuff off your face!'

I believe the guards knew only too well the detrimental effect on us of not only receiving such cruel treatment, but also having been forced to watch it inflicted on others. Our hatred for the guards and frustration at having to stand by and watch our small brothers and other young ones get hit for bed-wetting, fostered deep feelings of revenge. After his release, one boy from the Home tried to find out where one of the guards lived with the intention of killing him. Fortunately for him he was unable to locate the guard.

The punishment we received at Kinchela would be considered a criminal act by today's standards. The managers and the guards of places such as Kinchela would be facing court action. The boys that were taken away from their families and spent time in Kinchela were not the same boys when they came out. They would never be the same again.

*

Cruelty had a long history at Kinchela. In 1937, as reported in Bringing them Home, *the manager of Kinchela was investigated for extreme cruelty towards boys after complaints were made. In a memo from the Aboriginal Welfare Board the manager at the time was ordered not to whip the boys with a stockwhip and not to be drunk on duty (see P Read,* Stolen Generations and the Removal of Aboriginal Children in New South Wales 1883–1967*).*

Today, the treatment of the boys at Kinchela would be headlines, national news, the subject of current affairs programs and government enquiries. There would be an outcry from child protection groups, human rights organisations and anyone who cared.

*

Divide and conquer

Advice on problem solving: settle it with your fists.

These words of wisdom from the guards to young boys in their formative years caused many problems back then and later in our adult lives. In the Aboriginal culture that we knew, before we were taken, parents didn't beat children and we didn't beat each other. There were ways to settle disputes, and violence was not one of them.

We found out years later that it was deliberate government policy to alienate us from our natural families and all other Aboriginals. And that policy started from the time we woke in the morning until the time we fell into bed each night. We'd already been alienated from our families. Now it was time to create suspicion and ill-will within our own peer groups. The guards liked to see us fight amongst ourselves and did their best to encourage disagreements, making more of them than was necessary.

Some of the more serious disputes were settled by boxing.

'Get your gloves on,' Mr Pooley would say.

It didn't matter who won, lost or who got hurt during these enforced fights. They probably reasoned that while we battled against each other there was less chance of us uniting and causing any trouble as a group.

Confined in a hostile place of detention, sixty adolescent boys with issues of abandonment, rejection, anger, frustration and loneliness, coupled with emerging hormones, was a recipe for aggression. Small disagreements became bigger conflicts. We tried to stop each other from getting into trouble but too often we were in the position where we only had the time and opportunity to look after our brothers and ourselves.

It was always hard for the younger ones. The guards would try hard to keep us apart from our brothers during the course of the day. We all made an effort to help them through their trials, sneaking food to the smallest boys who were denied it due to bed-wetting. A Koori cook who came in on the weekends would often sneak a bit of food to a boy if he missed out on his meal. Helping each other in times of adversity made our connections with each other stronger, often outweighing the efforts of the guards to divide us, but it also made our lives difficult.

The efforts to pit us against each other started with the smallest boys. The guards went around the tables at meal times asking, 'Does anybody want any sweets?' Some of the little boys would eagerly raise their hands. The guard would saunter over to the boy and whisper in his ear, and occasionally the boy would whisper something back. Then he'd get a lolly. The boy may have told the guard that number eighty-four swore or that number six hadn't swept up properly. The guards groomed the young boys to tell tales on others.

Mr Pooley had an elite squad, known as the 'Bully Boys'. He would choose older, more aggressive boys and encourage them to bully others. If they didn't do what they were supposed to do, then they would be harassed themselves. Bully boys would take our meals and trip us up as we walked past them. Retaliation meant a beating. The inmates who were disliked by the guards became fair game for the bully boys, and life for them was miserable. Guards turned a blind eye or looked on with pleasure while all sorts of wrongdoing were carried out by the bullies.

Another method of divide and conquer was to employ a prefect system. Prefects were ordered to hit boys for menial things and to keep discipline if the guards weren't around. These prefects, to their credit, acted more like big brothers. The head prefect for a time was Harry Penrith (later to be known as Burnum Burnum). His younger brother was in the Home with us as well. Both in the Home and at Kempsey High, Harry was very popular.

Appearance-wise, Kinchela boys stood out from other boys at school and in the street and from other Koori school students. We were meant to stand out. The clothes we wore with our numbers stamped on them, the unfashionable soup-bowl haircuts they gave us, the slow hesitant walk mistreated children seem to acquire, the looks of despair on so many of the faces ensured we looked and acted differently to the other Koori children and Anglo-Saxon children. Almost as if we were something from side-show alley.

Some of the local kids were jealous that we had school shoes on when they didn't. They didn't know the only time we ever got to wear shoes was at school and only at school. As soon as we returned to the Home we were made to remove our shoes. Outside school hours you were caned if caught with your shoes on.

Some of the white students at high school hated us because they believed we were looked after better than they were. We had government-supplied school uniforms, but they didn't because their parents couldn't afford to buy them. I would have gladly swapped my uniform, shoes and lifestyle for the life of a local kid who lived with his mum and dad.

Our behaviour ensured we were alienated. Even the local town Kooris thought we were stuck up, because we didn't talk much. What they didn't know was we were under strict instructions from Mr Borland that under no circumstances were we to talk with or to make friends with the other Koori boys at the high school.

Mr Telfour, our teacher at the Kinchela school, had taught us that politeness was an essential value, and because we respected and liked him, we listened and took his advice. Kinchela boys generally were of a quiet nature. This was due mainly to our spirits being partially (and in some cases totally) broken by the authorities at the Home. When we were out on the street or attending high school, most of the boys adopted a subservient profile. We lived a life equivalent of juveniles who had broken the law and had been put in a very strict jail. The difference being, we were innocent. Mr Borland used the prefects to stay informed of any friendships being formed with other non-Kinchela Koori boys, and we soon learned which prefects to avoid.

I don't think the school headmaster had any knowledge of Mr Borland's rulings on friendships, because he always mixed us with outside boys for sports and other activities.

*

By the time I was fourteen, my school report sent to the Aboriginal Welfare Board said of me, 'Is lazy to the extreme and totally lacks ambition to improve himself.' In their eyes, 'improve himself' means assimilating, being more like a whitefella, thinking and behaving like one, and forgetting your Koori culture. As for laziness, in the Home they worked us like slaves, and I wasn't lazy in looking after my three younger brothers; I had to keep a look out for them constantly and take care of them the best I could. In school, it's true I wasn't interested in most subjects except for painting, art and science, and anyway, it was difficult to learn anything and concentrate properly when you're traumatised like we were.

There were many methods of alienating us from our own parents and culture.

One incident which left me extremely distressed occurred when I met up with my uncle at the Kempsey Show. The local show was one of the few events which we could attend. Once we were inside the showground we were broken up into small groups with a prefect assigned to each group. The prefect I was with let us go where we wanted, as long as we met him back where we started.

I headed straight for the sideshow alley, with the hope that my father would be there working in the boxing tents, and looked closely at each boxer along the line. Suddenly I stopped and went back to look at one in particular. I felt my spirits lift; my face broke out in a smile. Standing there, looking proud and strong, was my uncle Jim Simon.

Jim fought under the name 'Coogan Brown'. His nickname was 'Classy Coogan' and he was a highly regarded southpaw. He was flown over from Wellington in New South Wales to Wellington in New Zealand to fight for the British Empire title. In this period of his life Uncle Jim was saving his boxing earnings to buy a truck and tour Australia as a missionary. He took his bible to all his fights. He did almost ten kilometres of road work a day and trained in his home-made gym in his backyard.

Seeing him standing there in his silk boxing robe filled me with pride. My need for family, for someone who loved me and for a familiar face was so strong that I ran forward to the front of the stage shouting 'Uncle Jim...Uncle Jim', pushing past other spectators and jumping up and down in front of the stage. His arms were folded as he looked down at his lace-up boots, and then he saw me there in the front of the crowd. He jumped down and hugged me.

The feeling of being so close to a relative, someone who actually cared about me was overwhelming. I broke down in tears. He took me into the tent and I watched him fight and win. After the fight he came back and spent some time with me. He told me what he knew of the family and how Mum and Dad were. I told him about life at Kinchela and what was happening to my brothers and me. I remember him shaking his head but not saying too much. By that time I had already decided that my parents didn't want me, so I didn't ask my uncle why I had been taken. He didn't discuss the reason with me. It was too painful for him to talk about, and it wasn't part of our culture to discuss painful topics with children. We walked and talked and then the time came for me to return to the pick-up point, where he gave me a photo of himself boxing. I thought about escaping with him, but my brothers were back at the Home and I couldn't leave them.

As we said our goodbyes a rush of panic engulfed me. My past family life was flashing before me. Now the only contact with that life was about to leave me and I had no idea when and if I would ever see him again. When I was younger I used to see my uncles almost every day and it was taken for granted that life was meant to be that way. Tears flooded down my face, my nose started running and I couldn't control my sobbing. He was on his way back to his life and I was on my way back to mine. I was feeling the same feelings as when I had been taken from Platto.

That photograph was the only link with my previous life, and to my brothers and me it was the most important possession in the world. Back at Kinchela I was showing it to the other boys and telling them all about Uncle Jim when Mr Borland saw us huddled together.

'Give me a look at that photograph, thirty-three,' he said. I handed it up. He took one look at it and sneered.

'He's no good, he's just a drunk, he'll never amount to anything. You shouldn't be keeping photos of useless drunks.'

He shoved it back at me, crumpled and creased. The hurt shot through me. I was now embarrassed in front of the other boys, because I'd just told them about what a great fighter my uncle was and explained all the different things he had done during his career. I felt angry that the manager had insulted a man he knew nothing about.

This type of brainwashing was a daily occurrence. The guards told us constantly that our parents and relatives were no good and it was in our breeding to be evil.

'All blacks are a lying, thieving, low-life race of people,' we were told.

'Your only hope for improvement is to keep away from your own people,' they'd say.

Sometimes while we were studying, a guard would pass and say, 'You know your parents don't want youse, you little black bastards. That's why you're here.'

The fact that no relative had come to rescue us or to visit us gave some of us cause to think that maybe the guards were right. Even though the white man treated us cruelly, at least he kept us fed, clothed and gave us some sort of an education. This type of reasoning gave the guards fodder for reinforcing their ideas.

Occasionally letters arrived, but before they were handed over to any boy the manager or guards would open them and check the contents. Anything that looked like it might be of an affectionate nature, had a positive tone or talked about release was censored. Sometimes a boy would receive a letter with all the words except for about a dozen totally crossed out.

I had strong memories of how much my family loved us, but underneath there was the nagging thought that perhaps in reality they didn't. My brothers were still asking when Dad was coming to take us back. Most of the five- to nine-year-olds were constantly asking for their mums and dads, but generally the older boys tried not to let on just how much pain they were in. Whenever we inquired about our family we were told, 'Anyone who comes to the gate is allowed to visit, but no-one ever comes to the gate. Just get used to it.'

Many boys were told that their mother or their father (quite often both) were dead, when in fact they were alive. Being told Mum and Dad were dead caused many to suffer severe depression, which would go undiagnosed and untreated. Some boys lost all hope and just wanted to die. The guards delighted in delivering this news. We had no way of knowing that our parents didn't even know where we were. Sometimes an incident or a memory would spark off a cascade of emotions, which was always difficult to cope with.

I started making horses, cowboys and little Indian figures out of plasticine at the Home. The manager was so impressed with them he told one of his friends at the bank in Kempsey about them. They ended up in the bank's display window at Kempsey. I never received any pay or credit for them. I thought back to when I used to make cowboys and Indians out of clay back at Purfleet and Platts Estate when I was a small boy. My mother would say how good they were and put them around the house. I longed for praise, affection and for a normal family life.

After a couple of years, it became obvious to us that our parents weren't coming to get us. We never received any visits from our parents or relatives. We found out years later that all relatives were denied access to the Home. The State Archives File number 1/9812 — the 'Visitors Book' — from 1951 to 1962 shows the only visitors to Kinchela Boys' Home were Welfare Board staff, and others involved in the operation of the Home. Not one relative's name is entered in the book for that eleven-year period.

As time went on we believed more and more that our families didn't want us. We watched as older boys were released and quickly replaced with young ones. We watched as the same lies were perpetrated all over again. We suffered with them the emotional bombardment from the guards. And because we had to, we got tough. If we fell or hurt ourselves in any way, the only comfort we received was from the other boys. We were expected to get over whatever it was that ailed us, and because we were all in the same situation, compassion wasn't high on the list from most of the other boys anyway. They tried but were usually too busy trying to survive themselves.

It didn't happen overnight, but the indoctrination from the people in the Home had started to have an effect on me. I knew nothing of politics, government policies, Protection Boards or the history or the concept of eradicating a whole race. I only felt their effects. Angry feelings were growing inside of me. Certain thoughts were festering in my head; my parents had abandoned me. They were Aboriginal. Perhaps the guards were right. I reached the point where I started to hate my own race. Especially my mother.

Brothers, boils and breakout

My youngest brother Lenny arrived at Kinchela when he was five years old. He didn't remember me. He didn't remember David or Murray either. We were only small boys ourselves when we last saw him. Fortunately David and Murray were still in the young boys' dormitory where Lenny would be sleeping.

After processing, Lenny was sent to eat something. Being only five and having only just arrived, eating was the last thing on his mind. One of guards told me to go over and make him eat, so I approached him.

'I'm your brother Billy,' I said.

He looked at me blankly. I waited for some recognition but I knew then that to him I was a stranger. He had no memory of me at all.

By telling him he would get into trouble, I was eventually able to talk him into eating a few bits of food, but he was very distressed. I tried to pacify him by telling him that he had two other brothers at the Home there and that he would soon see them in the dormitory. He didn't respond. I went with him after his meal to his new quarters and introduced him to Murray and David, but there wasn't even a flicker of recognition. It took quite a while for him to accept that he had three brothers.

At least Lenny had brothers in the dormitory. When I was young I was my younger brothers' protector, but I was also fortunate enough to have an older boy in the Home who used to look out for me. If I ever had any trouble with any of the older boys that I couldn't handle, I used to tell my friend Eric and he would fix it up. I really needed and appreciated that, because I didn't feel so alone when I had problems. It was because of Eric's interest in my welfare that allowed me to be stronger for my brothers. Even the guards didn't mess with Eric, realising that his dominant position among the boys made the guards' jobs easier, if they kept him on side. Mr Borland was even civil to him. Now that I was older I hoped I could look out for Lenny.

I tried to stay healthy to look after my brothers, but there were times when ill health plagued me. I had a boil on my backside in a very awkward place. I waited until I was in pain before I said anything because sickness seemed to anger the manager and guards. I was taken to Kempsey Hospital, as the boil was infected. I went in the back of a truck, lying face down on my stomach. I remember thinking that the driver purposely went over every bump in the road.

Kempsey was a racist town in those times. Aboriginal people were prohibited from swimming in the same pool as whites. We couldn't sit at the same tables as them in a cafe or a restaurant either.

The doctor in Casualty took one look at me, and I could see by the expression in his eyes what he must have thought of me. A nurse pulled my legs apart and then I passed out. I thought about Job in the Bible and how he must have felt, only he had boils all over his body. I woke up in a hospital bed, my backside burning in pain. Soon after I was taken back to the Home, only with just as much pain as on the way in, maybe more. Traumatic times, such as going to hospital, are times that a child needs the comfort and support of a parent. We had no-one. In normal families a child returning from hospital would convalesce in front of the television or radio with ice cream. If Mr Pooley thought we were listening in to the radio in his room, he would turn it down or off.

I was nearly fifteen years old when I decided to run away. The weeks leading up to my decision had been particularly traumatic. I was continually in trouble for what seemed to be trivial matters, and was caned or put in detention. The cruelty and injustice were hard enough to bear, and the hypocrisy of the manager was just as difficult.

Mr Borland was a stickler for correctness and high morals, yet he would let his wife parade around in front of the older boys scantily clad. Then if they took notice of her he would cane them. It would have been obvious to Mr Borland that his wife's presence in a provocative state of dress was going to cause a problem with pubescent boys.

That week two boys were released to go back with their families as they had come of age. These boys came from South-West Rocks, where their father was employed as a fisherman. The Welfare Board must have thought it prudent that these two boys be uprooted from their family and moved fifteen kilometres to live with strangers. This insane decision angered me. I didn't mention it to anyone, but I was determined to escape.

Escaping was a very real consideration for those without brothers left behind. And for some, even a brother left behind wasn't enough to keep them there. Sometimes the problems a boy faced were insurmountable and he'd feel there was no alternative.

Years later I knew about the government Acts. In one of these documents it is stated that any child who runs away from a Home where they have been placed by the Board may be dealt with as a 'neglected' child and be dealt with by the Child Welfare Act. What a joke. I was running *from* neglect and abuse, but because I was running away from 'protection' I would be labelled as neglected. Some whitefella logic that is.

About one in the morning, after the night guard had made his rounds, I quietly made up my bed so that it looked like I was still there. Then I calmly walked out between the rows of beds, past Mr Pooley's room and out through the main entrance door of the dormitory. Once outside a rush of adrenaline poured into my system. Keeping to the shadows where possible, I ran across the compound, jumped over the fence into the work boys' paddock, and then jumped over another fence into a neighbouring farm. I ran across fields towards the main highway. The further away from the Home I ran, the more confident I became. Bitumen loomed up in front of me and I knelt down to catch my breath. I looked back in the direction I had come and could see no torches nor hear any voices. So far so good.

I turned towards Kempsey, approximately twenty kilometres south. The highway was quiet as I walked, keeping as close to the edge of the roadway as I dared. I had no idea how far my parents' home was or if it was possible to get there without being caught, but I had to try. Every time a car or truck came along, I hid in the bushes to avoid detection. Once my heart had stopped beating wildly and my breathing returned to normal, my thoughts turned to the consequences of being caught.

When boys ran away through the night, their departure was discovered early the next morning. Mr Borland never seemed to believe boys when they said they knew nothing of the runaway's plans. After an escape, the atmosphere at the Home was strained and everyone made sure they were on their best behaviour. We would stand and listen to Mr Borland's speech about the impending doom of the offender once caught. Jail was mentioned quite a bit and for most, the threat of being incarcerated was enough of a deterrent.

My already clouded mind was spinning with anxiety. How would Lenny, David and Murray get on without me? I regretted not saying goodbye to them, but I purposely didn't discuss my plan with them. This way they could honestly say to the manager when asked, that they didn't know where I was and had no knowledge of my intention to leave. Whether or not they would be believed would be up to the manager and the guards.

I had been gone now for about two and a half hours. I walked into Kempsey along through the main part of the shopping area when a police car approached. They didn't see me hiding behind a pylon. After they passed I started walking again. Walking and worrying. I got as far as the bridge. I thought about my brothers. Murray was twelve and could look after himself, but the two youngest could not. I slowed down. The future now held doubt. What if Mum and Dad didn't want me? What if they had forgotten me? Suddenly the escape seemed like a terrible mistake. I took a few more steps. Then I turned around and started walking back.

As I retraced my steps I tried to justify my decision. Someone had to take care of my brothers and I was the only one who could do it. They needed me. I tramped the twenty kilometres back to the Home. I knelt down near the hedge waiting until the guard did his rounds and then very quietly entered the dormitory. One of the boys looked up as I passed his bunk, but didn't recognise anything was amiss. I took my pillow and extra blankets out from under the covers, put my pyjamas on and climbed into bed as if nothing had happened. I was asleep for about an hour and a half, when the prefects came to wake us up. I never mentioned my escape to anyone. That way I was sure the manager would never find out about it.

Soon it was back to broken rules and broken skin. Mr Borland had many canes, thick and thin, but he favoured the thick ones. Sometimes when I knew I was to be caned, I'd spit on my hands and then rub it into my eyes so that he would think I was crying, in the hope he'd give me less strokes. I left his office once after being caned with a thin cane and I went down to Murray who was down in the yard raking the lawn. I told him about what I'd done to make it look like I was already crying, and then I started to laugh. Mr Borland heard me and called me back up to the office, and when I came out of his office this time I really was crying.

The anger and frustration that were building up inside me only became exacerbated when I watched my peers suffering because of rules that were impossible to keep. One such rule was eating everything on the plate. One evening, twins Perry and Joel were at the dinner table. As Perry felt ill, he wasn't eating. A guard saw the unfinished food and demanded that it be eaten. His twin tried to explain about Perry not feeling well, but the guard stood there until Perry forced the food down and, satisfied, the guard walked away. Two seconds later Perry vomited up his meal. The boys at the table made the appropriate horrified comments, attracting the guard's attention. Joel quickly scooped up the vomit and ate it so Perry wouldn't be beaten. There was total silence at the table. The lengths that boys would go to protect each other, especially their brothers, was something that has stayed with me all my life.

The months dragged on and Santa, snow and reindeers began to appear on shop windows. The youngest boys were having their first Christmas in the Home. Toys were only given out at Christmas time. The older boys looked on with displeasure as the toys were given out; they knew that on Boxing Day afternoon, all the presents had to be handed back to the guards and put back into storage until the next year, when they would be given out again. These presents were not given because we were loved or cared about by anyone; it was just a ritual. The toys given to us at Christmas were donated by charity. I couldn't really imagine Mr Borland going out to buy gifts for us. Much like Christmas, birthdays were a non-event.

Once a year we were given new clothes, fresh bed linen and good food. It wasn't Christmas; it was Aboriginal Welfare Inspectors visiting week. We were ordered to be on our best behaviour or else. We were young but we weren't stupid; all the attention thrust upon us by the guards while the inspectors were there came to a sudden halt soon as they left. There were no beatings while the inspectors were there, but as soon as their car had left the premises, it was back to beatings. Punishment parade, suspended for the visiting period, started up again at four o'clock.

The end of the year was also the time when the manager would read out boys' school report cards in front of everyone. Your grades determined what punishment was meted out to you. A bad report meant a caning. A mediocre one meant extra kitchen duty or a ban on sport and swimming. If our reports were satisfactory then nothing was said. Even if our reports were very good, nothing was said. Praise was an alien concept.

It was crushing not to have good work acknowledged, no matter what type of work it was. When I was a work boy, a boy named Mitchell and I had to bring cows from the dairy down to South-West Rocks on a road that was flooded and in pouring rain. It was one of the most difficult things we had to do in our time there, but by sheer determination and whips we herded cattle for miles, quite an accomplishment for two teenage boys. We felt proud of ourselves, but we had to be content with congratulating each other.

As I grew older my aggressive tendencies started to surface. I took my aggression out on people whom I perceived were against me, and I also took it out against others on the sports field. Practical jokes were my other tendency.

One weekend the guards took us to the old Trial Bay Gaol where there were two trees hanging over the edge of a very high cliff. I decided to give one of the boys a bit of a push, as I knew he'd grab onto the trees because they were right there in front of him, but he'd be sure to get a big fright. I called Tim over and while he looked over the edge I gave him a push. He latched on to a tree and yelled and swore at me.

Later, when we all went down to the beach for a swim, I looked into a nearby rock pool and saw an octopus. I called out to Tim.

'Tim, over `ere. `Ave a look at this!'

Tim came over and bent down on his knees to look.

'What've ya found?' he asked.

I pushed his face into the rock pool, the octopus latched on to it and he ran along the beach screaming while I laughed. Other boys pulled the octopus off his face.

'I'm gonna kill ya when I grow up!' he said.

At school Science was my best subject, but I undertook dangerous pranks with chemicals. Despite being punished I found I needed to play practical jokes. I wanted attention, acceptance. I wanted to be someone.

I had been a work boy for about a year when Mr Borland left. We were happy about this until his replacement arrived. Mr Worthington was a big man with a big temper. My first encounter with him arose because one of the guards hit my brother Lenny quite savagely. I decided to go and ask about what Lenny had done to deserve such a beating, even though asking was against the rules. The guard didn't like the way I spoke to him so he went and told the new manager that I was being rude.

'You want to act like a man, I'll belt the hell out of you like a man,' was one of his favourite sayings.

He said this before he swung a punch at me. I ducked and missed it and then anger overtook me. I punched him hard in the stomach and then I ran. Just as I got to the Kinchela shop, the police came along. It was Sergeant Reed and he was a good man. I had helped him out by volunteering to cut grass and pick up stones in the work gangs. He pulled up and told me to get in.

'You been playing up, Bill?' he asked.

I didn't say anything. He drove me back to the Home, where Worthington told the police officer that he wanted me charged.

I was taken to South-West Rocks Jail and charged with assault. I was put in a cell for the night. In the morning Reed gave me some breakfast, and later that day I attended Kempsey courthouse with him. Outside the courthouse, the Sergeant said to me, 'If you apologise to Mr Worthington, he said you can go back to the Home.'

Not for one second did I want to apologise to Mr Worthington for anything, but I had to think about my brothers and how they relied on me to look after them. I would be no good to them in jail, so I decided I would have to apologise.

I wasn't sorry for what I had done, but that wasn't important. I apologised to Mr Worthington, he accepted my apology, and I was taken back to the Home. I was lucky that I had the chance to apologise and not have to front up to the magistrate, because by 1963, the year I hit the manager, the Children's Court had taken over many areas that the Board had dealt with, and I may have been sent to a juvenile detention centre.

*

From 1943, those deemed 'uncontrollable' by the Children's Court came under the Child Welfare Department and were sent to state corrective institutions. For more details see Bringing Them Home. National Inquiry into the Separation of Aboriginal and Torres Strait Islander Children from Their Families, *Human Rights and Equal Opportunity Commission, 1997, p. 48.*

*

'If you don't behave yourself, things are going to be very, very difficult for you,' was all Mr Worthington said once we were in the car.

When I got back to the Home, the younger boys cheered me, never expecting to see me again. This incident increased my respect among the boys and even the guards seemed to leave me alone. For a while I felt good. I wanted to be liked if I couldn't be loved.

Before I left the Home permanently I received a letter from my mother. It didn't say much. Most of the text had been blacked out. If I had been able to read the censored part, I would have known that my father had died.

As I got older and went to high school I was able to get away from the Home a bit more by taking up sports played against other schools. I travelled to country towns with the football team, even though I wasn't the most enthusiastic player. I always played the position of wing in the under-eighteens, probably since I could run fast because my legs were so skinny.

Another way of getting out of the Home was to be involved in manual labour in the local community. Sergeant Reed from South-West Rocks recruited workers for heavy work such as clearing fields and picking up rocks in the grounds of the Kempsey Hospital. Rather than stay at the Home, boys as young as seven, eight and nine would volunteer to pick up rocks all day in the boiling hot sun and cut long grass with a scythe. This was terribly hard on their young bodies and dangerous as well but it was still better than staying at the Home and living in fear of cruelty and punishment that could be round the corner at any time.

Some of the work boys were permitted to be members of the local lifesavers, down at South-West Rocks. By the time I left school and became a work boy, we were no longer allowed to join them. I believe the manager stopped us joining the club because he could see we were enjoying ourselves there. It seemed that the only time I was met with kindness was when I went away from the Home.

Sunday mornings meant compulsory church attendance. The Church of England minister was so uninteresting he made you want to sleep. On Sunday afternoons the Catholic priest would come out, and my brothers and I would attend again. The priest had wine, the real stuff. In between giving up sips from a cup, he drank most of it himself and would be somewhat inebriated by the end of the service.

I remember the three of us would draw straws to see who would help the priest out to the car with all of his belongings. It was the winner's job to filch some cigarettes out of his bag on the way to the car. The priest was so tipsy he never noticed. Once in possession of the cigarettes it was off to the toilet to smoke them without getting caught by the guards.

Twice a year Mr Hermann came to the boys' home, the same man who used to come to the mission at Purfleet when I was a child. He'd tell us stories and play his piano accordion. It reminded me of life with my family at Purfleet. Mr Hermann would go to the missions at Narrabri, Moree, Cootamundra, Cowra, Purfleet, Burnt Bridge, Pilliga Scrub and many others. While he was there he'd always take photos and slides, so he could show the children in the other missions. Sometimes we'd see some of our relatives, or people we knew in his photos. Mr Hermann never let on that he knew us from his visits to our communities in times past, but I think he recognised us. He was a very welcome sight when he came and sorely missed when he left.

People like Mr Telfour and Mr Hermann were our only reminder that kind and caring people existed in white society. Skin colour, age, background and social status were not platforms on which they judged us. They respected us as fellow human beings, bringing small slices of happiness to lives of despair.

As time progressed at Kinchela I started to believe that what we were told about our parents must be true. I became consumed with rejection. Later, as a high school and work boy I could feel the aggression building up inside. I had the image of my mother turning her back and walking away churning inside my head. I had yelled out for her to help. She didn't care. She let those welfare people take us away and she never came to take us back. I hated her.

After eight years my release day finally came. One morning Mr Worthington informed me that I was going to work for some fella in Sydney. I was to leave in four days with Matthew, another boy. There was no farewell party, no words of good wishes for the future, no presents or cards, nothing. I had mixed feelings: elation at being released, sadness about leaving my brothers. I had a talk to Murray about being responsible for the other two, as he was now the eldest brother still at the Home. By this time Murray was about fourteen, David was around twelve and Lenny was ten years old. I kept reassuring my brothers that they'd be all right and I promised I would come back and visit them. I think they knew that I'd never be able to do that.

The other boys were happy for Matthew and me, and we were very excited. We laughed because we were going to be free, and we cried because we knew we were about to be separated from our brothers and we didn't know when we would be together again.

Finally, departure day arrived. We were given our sealed files, some small change and our tickets to Sydney. Mr Worthington gave us some last-minute advice before sending us out into the world.

We boarded the train and as it pulled away from the station it was if a giant weight had been lifted from my shoulders, not completely, but I definitely felt a lot easier. The further south we headed the more excited Matthew and I became. His time in the Home had had its problems as well, and he was also leaving behind a brother.

I could barely believe it; after all this time I was finally free. To me it was the greatest feeling, knowing I would be able to do as I wanted and not as I was told. Everything appeared to us in a different light. We saw things, normal everyday things, but through different eyes. The cows looked special, the people looked friendly, the places we passed through appeared interesting. Everything looked and felt different. That's because we were free. There was however a small cloud on my picture of perfection... we were scared, neither of us had been out in society like this before, unsupervised and with no one to tell us what to do. It was a big change for both of us, and although we didn't let on to one another, each of us knew the other was a bit frightened.

After many hours the train finally pulled in at Central Station and I walked into my new life, the last words of Mr Worthington beating in my brain.

'Remember, thirty-three, black people are the scum of the earth.'

LOST

Bikies, bashings and boys behind bars

We sat on the end of our beds and stared at each other. We didn't know what to do. The year was 1964, I was seventeen and I was free. Free to actually say what I was thinking, without a guard overhearing and hitting me. Free to earn my own money and to spend it as I saw fit. Free to come and go as I pleased and do what I wanted to do and not what I was told to do. Only people that have been denied their liberty can truly understand.

Matthew and I were in Bankstown in Sydney to work. Coming to terms with the realisation that we were free was a strange process. The beds were soft, the garage was quite comfortable and we were wearing clothes without numbers. But still we didn't know what to *do*. We didn't know how to be free.

A man from the welfare department had met us at the station and took us out to Bankstown. It had been arranged for us to stay with a German family in a converted garage behind their house.

For a while we didn't go anywhere. We knew no-one in Bankstown and neither of us knew where to go anyway. Mr Worthington had told us that if we wanted to get anywhere in life then we had to stay away from blacks. There didn't seem to be any other Kooris around the place. Underneath, we were scared. Free to go where ever we wanted, but too scared to do so. After a few days we ventured out as far as a walk around the block. We found a cafe nearby and started going there regularly for a soft drink, but that was as far as we went for the first few weeks.

A man from welfare came out to see us occasionally, and at first we were afraid that he might tell us we had to return to Kinchela. He asked us if we were all right and told us to make sure that we looked after our flat. He gave us directions to a place in town where we would be given our winter clothes. The German man who owned the house was questioned about our behaviour and must have given us a good report, because there were no repercussions. It took about six months to stop being anxious about being sent back.

We lived in the garage but ate our meals at the same table as the people who owned the house. We also showered in their bathroom, and more than once they told us how shy and well-mannered we were. It was almost as if they were surprised at how well-behaved we were. They had no idea we were raised in fear and punishment, but our quiet behaviour made it easier for them to accept us.

Our room and board for the week was £5 and our weekly wage was £7. That left us with £2 to ourselves, which seemed like a fortune. It was the first time we had ever had any real pocket money.

We were employed making box trailers for a company. Our boss, Arthur, seemed to be a decent man, and as long as we started work at the correct time and did our job properly, he was happy. After we'd been there a while, he gave Matthew and me a bible each. It was one of the first presents I'd received since I was a small boy, and I was very grateful.

We went regularly to the café because it was close to home and was different from any other place we'd been. We became good friends with the owner's son and the three of us often went into town on the train. Our new friend showed us Sydney; within no time we were going to dances and venturing up to Kings Cross. It was here that I was introduced to the self-medicator called grog. I had my first bottle of spirits.

Grog became an important part of all my social outings, but I didn't end up having the good time that the advertisements promised. When I was intoxicated I always thought about Kinchela, and I would find myself dredging up unpleasant and violent incidents and situations I had been a part of, or witnessed.

With increasingly morose thoughts I would sink into feelings of anger and sorrow. More grog fuelled thoughts of my brothers left behind. I pictured them lining up on the parade without me, frightened and alone. The more I thought about it, the angrier I became, and the angrier I was, the more I drank.

A local bikie gang used to drink at a hotel not too far from where we lived, and Matthew and I started drinking there too. I wanted to be part of this group but I didn't have a motorbike. I started dressing like the bikies and went some of their parties. Some of their ways were totally alien to me, but I tried to fit in with them. When they were drunk, so was I. And when they engaged in anti-social behaviour, I did too. On Saturday nights I'd go up to the Cross on the backs of their bikes and pick fights with other people. At first I found it distasteful fighting with others for no good reason, but grog quickly killed any moral argument I had with my conscience.

By now I was drinking very heavily on the weekends, from Friday evening until Sunday afternoons. I remained sober for work from Monday until Friday, but as soon as work was over for the week, the weekend was a blur of grog and anti-social incidents.

At night Matthew and I would often lie in our beds yarning about Kinchela and our brothers who were still there. Feelings of guilt consumed me at times. I was free while my brothers were still captives. These feelings manifested themselves in physical violence. I was angry. Angry at Kinchela, angry with white people and probably most of all, I was angry with myself for not being there for my younger brothers. Grog seemed to make life easier. It enabled me to get rid of the aggression that built up during the week, but at the time I never realised that I had a problem with it. Bashing people — white people — became an acceptable tonic for both Matthew and me.

Each week Matthew saved as much of his wage as possible, and eventually had enough to buy an F J Holden. That car quickly became his pride and joy, and most of his spare time was spent washing and polishing. We pooled money for petrol and spent many hours driving around the suburbs, getting more and more adventurous each day. His car gave us the independence we needed, and after a few months we discussed the possibility of going on a journey. This wasn't to be just any journey; we were planning a trip back to Kinchela Boys' Home to see our brothers. We had anxiety about this trip; it occurred to both of us that the manager might make us stay there, but because both Matthew and I missed our brothers desperately we knew we had to go. Together we calculated how much money we would need for the trip and then for the next month or two we saved as much of our wages as we could.

After seven weeks of judicious saving the weekend of our very first expedition arrived. Full of anticipation we left Sydney early on the Friday and drove directly to the outskirts of Kempsey. Uncomfortable seats and anticipation kept us awake for most of the night.

At about eight-thirty on the Saturday morning we made our way out to Kinchela. Memories were washing over me; things that I had put to the very back of my mind since leaving now dominated my thoughts. The closer to Kinchela we drove the angrier I became. Apprehension gave way to bravado and revenge.

We drove up to the compound, and straight away we knew we wouldn't be allowed to enter. Not deterred, Matthew decided to drive up the side fence between the Home and the farm next door. Halfway along the fence we stopped and then whistled for one of the boys to come over. Once he was in earshot I told him to go and get Lenny, David, Murray and Matthew's brother Robert.

As other boys saw us, they too came running over to the fence. We hadn't expected that we'd be so popular. The small boys talked excitedly and the older boys were firing questions at us quicker than we could answer. Our brothers were pushing to get near the fence. Soon we were all crying and laughing together. Our brothers told us bits of information about Kinchela life, and we told them about our new home and jobs. The amount of noise around us ensured we'd be noticed by the guards. Sure enough, about a quarter of an hour after we first pulled up, two guards came over and ordered everyone to get away from the fence. The boys didn't hear the guards at first as they were too busy talking, but when the guards got close enough they started hitting. It took only two minutes before all had left. As we said our goodbyes, I quickly slipped Murray some money.

The guards told us to leave straight away or they'd call the police. I was too depressed to answer them back. All the anger had gone. Matthew and I returned to the car, tears streaming down our cheeks as we drove away from Kinchela. All of our bravado and high spirits had given way to despair. The tears on David's and Lenny's faces as they waved goodbye were etched into my brain and haunted me for quite some time after. I felt guilty for months.

As we drove into Kempsey neither of us spoke, preferring to be left to our own thoughts. It was only Saturday lunchtime, but we were so downhearted we didn't need to discuss what to do for the rest of the weekend. We both just wanted to get as far away from Kinchela as possible. The rest of the day was spent returning to Sydney in silence. Regrets for both of us were so severe that never again were we tempted to return to Kinchela to visit our brothers.

With the bikies now firm friends, I spent all of my spare time frequenting dances, hotels and anywhere else I could find to get into trouble. A good night was one where I could get into a fight. One weekend at a dance in Bankstown, I was asked to leave as I was drunk and aggressive. After arguing about it with one of the organisers I went outside and retaliated by smashing their front window with my fist. Within minutes the police arrived and I was taken first to Bankstown Jail and then transported out to Long Bay Jail, where I was to be held on remand.

Four days later my case was heard. My boss spoke up for me, telling the magistrate that I was a reliable worker and that he would keep me on the right track in future. He also said he would pay the £70 damage I had caused to the window. The magistrate was satisfied, so although convicted, I was released into my employer's care.

While in Long Bay that first time I was reunited with my cousin Boxy. I hadn't seen him since I was taken from Platto. It seemed like a lifetime since he and I had cut ferns for the butcher up at Kendall. One morning Boxy looked at me for a long time.

'Your dad's dead,' he said.

That's how I found out that my father had died. He said my Dad had died at Hexham, while crossing the bridge. He'd been on his way home when he slipped and fell. This news put me into a severe depressive state. I had not yet returned, but in my imagination Mum and Dad would still be at Platto, and I would see them when I turned eighteen. Until then I would need permission from the Welfare Board to go anywhere.

Later in my life I would spend much more than four days in Long Bay. In total I would spend five years in jail. In 1979 I was sentenced to three years for armed robbery, and I did other stretches that amounted in total to another two years. My cousin Boxy and I had plenty of time to catch up when we were in jail together at various times. Thankfully, he showed me the ropes and kept a close eye on me. He told the other prisoners that they'd better leave me alone or else, and so no-one harmed me while I was there.

I remember at the time thinking that being in jail wasn't so bad. The men in jail had it a lot better than we did back in the Home. Once again I had a number, but there was much more freedom and the guards were less harsh. A broken rule might mean a hit over the ear, just like in the Home, but the guards in jail never hit nearly as hard as the Kinchela guards. There was no such thing as rehabilitation or any counselling or programs to try and understand why we were messed up and why we had committed crimes.

After the court case Matthew and I moved into a two-storey flat, which we shared with another family. The rent was cheaper, we had extra money and more freedom. Meals and showers could now be taken whenever we liked. We bought a record player, lamps and furniture to make the flat more homely.

It was here that I started to think about Redfern, as I had heard that some of my relatives were there. It took me some time before I could put names and faces together, but I was connected to my family again within a short time of arriving there. I found relatives who had lived at Purfleet when I was growing up. I heard that Mum was now living out at Wellington. I thought about this for a few days, and eventually told my boss about my mother and asked if I could go and see her. He seemed to understand, and said I could take two weeks holiday. It was agreed that I start holidays the following Friday.

Before I left to start my journey, I made a small gun out of scraps of metal. Using a lathe, I fashioned some pipe for a barrel and a grip from some plate steel. When it was finished it looked to me like a normal handgun. I made a shoulder holster to keep it in and I started wearing it around that night. No-one was going to give me trouble.

The train to Wellington left on the Saturday morning and I arrived at the station wearing a three-piece suit with a studded belt around my waist. I was sitting in the carriage wearing my new gun and as I leaned back the people sitting opposite me saw it under my coat. I felt really good when I saw them talking amongst themselves. I felt important.

Arriving at Wellington station, I asked the local cab driver if he knew where any members of the Simon family would be. He told me that they were all down by the Bell River, and I had him take me out there. He dropped me off as close as he could. To get to where my family was located I had to walk across a paddock, which was covered in burrs, long grass seeds and cow manure. By the time I got down to the riverbank my trousers were a mess, covered in burrs, prickles and dust.

This walk towards the creek was the beginning of a new phase of my life and, for better or worse, I needed to move forward.

Reunion

Stepping carefully over the broken beer and wine bottles, I made my way to the creek bank. Barking dogs and children yelling greeted me. I could see eight or nine grown-ups sitting under the tree, oblivious to all the shattered glass surrounding them, the noise from the children and the dogs. As I walked towards them I saw my Uncle Jim stand up. With a look of curiosity he walked over to me. He squinted and stared, trying to remember who I was, and then his face broke into a smile.

'Billy's 'ere...Billy's 'ere!' he shouted.

He walked up to me and gave me a firm handshake and a long hug. Others stood up and came over to me. Some were hugging me, others pumping my hand up and down and someone was patting me hard on my back. It seemed that almost everyone there knew me. I had relatives all around the camp; my grandfather was there as well. Most of them were my mother's family. I was re-introduced to my other uncles and cousins, not seen since childhood. They lived in humpies along the riverbank.

I asked about Mum and they told me she had remarried and was now living at a place on the other side of town. Uncle Jim said he'd take me over there to see her after we'd had a drink first. I sat down for what turned out to be quite a session, then after too many drinks Uncle Jim and I walked into town.

Just inside the town limits we hailed a taxi and went over to my mother's house. I paid the cab fare while my uncle walked to the door and knocked loudly. My Mum opened the door and Uncle Jim pointed behind at me.

'Do you know this fella 'ere?' he asked.

My mother stared at me, trying to place my face.

'No...no I don't.'

My uncle laughed and said, 'It's Billy...your son Billy, he's come 'ome to us.'

How come she doesn't know me? What happens now? Will she kiss me hello or tell me to leave? My emotions were running wild. I spoke first, as I stepped forward and bent over to kiss her.

'Hello Mum.'

I think she would have only just heard me. My voice had no strength in it at all. My throat was dry; the sound came out all weak and cracked. I could see she still wasn't sure who I was, but she gave me a kiss on the cheek anyway. We went inside and sat down at the table. My mother offered us a cup of tea. I could see the turmoil on her face. It was a difficult situation, and it took many cups of tea and a lot of yarning before she slowly realised that I was indeed her first-born.

The day moved on and the atmosphere cleared. We talked about many different things. When I began to feel comfortable with her I steered the conversation towards the time of our removal. She bent her head forward as she told me how she felt the day we were taken. She was crying as she explained that my father was grief-stricken, and as soon as the court case was over he left in despair to return to the boxing tents. She waited for him to return, but he never came back. After he went, there was nothing left for her at Platto but sadness, so she went out to Wellington to visit her father. I listened quietly with tears in my eyes, trying not to interrupt her. I had so many questions.

'I wrote you boys so many letters when I found out where you were, but you never replied,' she said. 'So I stopped writing.'

Her every word cut into my soul. Her tears spilled onto the table as she whispered that she wasn't even sure that we were still at Kinchela until Uncle Jim told her that he'd seen me at the Show.

'I thought by then you had forgotten all about me.'

Tears ran down my face. We sat up late yarning about the past, but even then I knew that I would never be able to accept the fact that she didn't try to save us on that winter's morning so long ago. I realised that no matter what my mother said to me, I just couldn't reconcile myself to our abandonment. I couldn't relate to my mother as a son.

This plagued me for most of my adult life, and I was never to have the proper mother-and-son relationship I should have had. I just couldn't forgive her for not trying to do something that day we were taken. What I didn't understand was tribal tradition. I had had no contact with my own culture and knew nothing of its workings. When a traumatic event takes place in Biripi culture and women are left powerless, they look away. This is done to hide the grief and feelings of helplessness. Even after I became aware of this tradition, I still blamed her for our captivity.

Those first couple of days at Wellington saw me drink more than I had ever drunk before. I was camping with my uncles and we were drinking most of the time. It seemed to be the normal way of life for them.

One afternoon, when I wasn't feeling too good from too much grog and not enough food, my uncles prepared a fire while some of the others went out and caught a goanna. After the fire was reduced to coals, my uncle threw on a freshly caught four-foot goanna, turning it occasionally until it was cooked. More drinking and revelry took place, until finally it was ready for eating, and because I was the guest they gave me what was considered to be the best part.

My uncle carefully broke off a leg for me and I cautiously bit into it, only to be surprised at how wonderful it tasted. That goanna was a good introduction to my lost culture.

In the following days I had many long conversations with my uncles and my mother. I really needed information about my father. I wanted to know what had happened to him, since I saw him at Kempsey all those years ago. I had asked Mum, but she said my Uncle Jim would be the best one to talk with, so I waited until Uncle Jim and I were both sober at the same time and then I asked him what I desperately needed to know.

He sat and considered for a few minutes, then he started talking. He told me that after his children were taken away, my father was never the same again. He couldn't cope with the loss and so he had left. The Show season was in full swing, so he caught up with his boxing troupe and worked the Shows for a few months. By this time the relationship between my parents had broken down and he and Mum had separated. She was living out in Wellington with her father.

I asked about his death and I asked not to be spared the truth. Reluctantly at first, Jim said that my Dad died senselessly after a prank went horribly wrong. He was on his way back from Ash Island when he was told that his kids were home. He asked my cousin if he was sure, and after being told that he was, my Dad took off. He started running along the highway on his way home to Platts Estate. When he got to the Hexham bridge he, like all the other Kooris, crossed over the Hunter River by running along the pipeline, parallel to the road — something he often did. Nearing the Hexham side of the pipeline, he slipped and fell onto the riverbank, leaving him cut and injured. He was rushed to Newcastle Hospital, but died later on that same day. We boys were still at Kinchela, and my father had died because of a joke gone wrong. When I think of him running along that highway, anxious to see his kids, I am overwhelmed.

Over the next few days my uncles told me many stories about my Dad and my family and about Koori life in general. For me this was an important time of learning.

My relationship with my mother was strained. I was experiencing mixed feelings about her. I both loved her and hated her too. We weren't spending much time together. Added to this, I didn't like her new husband, Steve, with whom she had had more children. I liked my new sisters and brothers and got on well with them, but there was a certain amount of jealousy in me. I argued with Steve quite a bit, especially when he had been drinking. He said hurtful things about my father and I think he resented me because I was a link between my mother and her former life. He hadn't met my Dad, but he'd obviously heard a lot about him from my uncles. He seemed to get on well with my four uncles and they spent a lot of time together. I was more at ease with my uncles.

My uncles lived over near the Chinese market gardens and they worked there most days as casuals. My money had run out about ten days after I had arrived and so I started work in the gardens. My uncles knew the job well and worked much faster than I could; I'd follow two or three rows behind them. After a while I became more skilled and kept up with them, chatting and laughing as we worked.

The time had come for me to return to Sydney. I had been gone three months. I said goodbye to my mother, but I felt more emotion when I said goodbye to my uncles. There was a wedge between my mother and me and we both knew it. It wasn't discussed but it was there, hanging like a thick curtain. We made efforts but they just didn't seem to work. We had no reference points, we had not shared experiences with each other, and so there was little to keep us together. With my uncles I felt at ease. We worked together, sat around drinking and yarning, laughing and eating. We could talk about the past and my father. I wondered if I would ever be able to communicate with my mother on the same level.

My boss wasn't too happy with me when I turned up unannounced after three months. All I could tell him was that most of my relatives were out at Wellington and we had so much catching up to do that time had just gotten away from me. He thought about it for a while then decided to give me another go. I started work again the very next day.

*

According to correspondence in the files of the Aboriginal Welfare Board, the Board considered charging Bill with absconding. His boss's letter stated however that he was a good worker, polite and personable. His boss understood his need to be with his people and would give him another chance.

*

Matthew was still there painting trailers, however he had moved from the flat we shared with me to live in another flat above a shop. He wasn't too impressed that I had been away for so long and had not contacted him, but I think he understood my need to be with my relations and to catch up on all the things I'd missed out on for so many years. I moved in with him and soon settled down to life in Bankstown again, only now I was more aware of a different kind of life.

On the weekends I'd go into Redfern to see my other relations. I was beginning to make new friends around there and feel comfortable. There were four or five other Kinchela boys there, so I felt at home. I found my Auntie Maree there (my father's first cousin) and she and I got on really well together. Unfortunately, though, I could only go into Redfern on the weekends and that just wasn't enough time to spend with everyone. So about eight months after I returned from Wellington I left my job to go and live at Redfern full time.

At that time I had a strong need to live among my relations. I didn't know why I had this urge. Auntie Maree was happy for me to live at her house. Since I had returned from Wellington, Matthew and I seemed to have grown apart. He was never comfortable going to Redfern, and so we went our separate ways.

I was now just on twenty years old, alone in the world, with a full-blown addiction to grog, no money and itchy feet. It had taken less than a year for me to turn into an alcoholic. My itchy feet led me to move from Redfern out to La Perouse, where there were quite a few Kinchela boys living. I felt the need to live with people who had been part of my past, who I felt at home with. I didn't know why I had this need but it was strong.

Life was very different once I left the safety of Auntie Maree's house. There was no accommodation for me at La Perouse, so I lived in an old abandoned car on a dump. The car shell became my very own home and my first car. I felt good about living like this; although I lived rough, it was a place I could call my very own. Life was good. During the day another man and I used to go up to the golf course and collect lost golf balls for which the golf club would give us money. While the money we made from this was enough to buy food, it limited us to a menu of hot chips and bread and Devon. The other way we made money was to dive for coins that the tourists would throw while they watched us 'natives'. The money we earned never stretched to buying clothes, so at night we'd go 'snowdropping' — stealing clothes off other people's clotheslines.

After a while the restrictions of living in a bomb car and daily diving for coins lost their appeal and so, all decked out in recently acquired 'snowdropped' clothes, I went back to Redfern to live on The Block.

Goin' down

Any addiction requires a source of ready cash. Some casual employment that I had found at the Yellow Pages had ended, and trying to limit grog to the weekends was becoming difficult. I was desperately trying to lead a normal life, to get back on track and to stop drinking but it was just too hard. Temptation was everywhere; there were too many others around who invited me to join them during the day.

I found new sources of money. Stealing it and extorting it. I needed money for grog and for the two-up games, and these methods proved easy for me. I'd go out with others to the edge of The Block and deliberately pick a fight with anyone walking along the footpath. Then, after knocking him down, we'd take his money.

We'd often go up to Kings Cross and 'roll' people up there for the money in their pockets. We'd knock them down, steal their money and take off back to Eveleigh Street where we knew we'd be safe; the police were cautious about coming onto The Block. There was a hamburger van that would park up near Redfern railway station till late at night, and we often ordered food and then ran off without paying.

Food wasn't a priority but grog was, and that's where the money went. When I couldn't find work, stealing money became normal practice. Even though I had a bed at Aunty May's place, I often stayed out most of the night, spending my stolen money on drinking and gambling. Through the day, my friends and I would stop to sleep anywhere we found convenient, usually under a tree or at a relative's place.

During the week we had very little available food to eat, but on Sundays we'd go down to the Aboriginal Foundation at Central. There we could get a proper meal and a cup of tea for free. They also had a band as well as a few snooker tables. It was a change from on The Block, and it guaranteed us at least one good meal for the week.

While I was living with my Aunty Maree, more often than not I'd get home very late, and she'd already have locked up and gone to bed. I didn't want to wake her so I'd sleep in the flowerbed in her front yard, even in winter, with only the flowers to stop the wind.

Many ex-Kinchela boys drifted toward Redfern, and sometimes there would be quite a few of them there at any one time. One night I arrived at the pub, and standing down one end of the bar was my brother Murray. Finding him there was overwhelming for both of us. We stomped and shouted and hugged each other. I bombarded him with questions without giving him a chance to answer a single one. He told me about David and Lenny and how they were surviving. I was glad the boys were all right, but I didn't want to know any more about the Home.

The first news I gave him was that Dad had died. I told him how and when it happened. Then I told him Mum had remarried and was living out at Wellington not far from our uncles Jim, Gilbert, Kevin and Nick.

Murray stayed on in Redfern doing casual work, but he decided that he needed to see his mother, and because I was feeling restless I agreed to go with him. At this time I was a very heavy drinker and gambler managing to hold down some casual jobs. I had no money and had to bash someone for money for the tickets the night before we left.

*

When we arrived I took Murray over to see Mum and introduced him to her. She looked at him and they hugged and she cried a bit but I could see that she had only a faint memory of him. Murray was having the same trouble as I had. He could barely remember her at all. He was only seven when he was taken and there just hadn't been enough time for him to bond with her. They were more like acquaintances than mother and son. He stayed with her for a month while I went to work around the Mudgee area. I was earning good money at that time but my wages went on drink at the Coolah pub. With all the money I earned I could have bought a car.

On arriving back at Wellington I asked Murray if he wanted to come out to Gulargambone with me to see our uncles who'd moved out there. He was more than ready to leave our stepfather's house, so I packed a rifle for rabbit hunting and we hitched to Gulargambone. There we found my uncles Jim, Kevin, Gilbert and Nate. We stayed six months with them at Gulargambone, living mainly on birds and rabbits.

Most days were spent drinking anything we could get our hands on. I was drinking methylated spirits with a bit of boot polish added in for flavour. We drank metho whenever we couldn't get our hands on grog, because it was cheap. After a while I stopped adding the boot polish and drank it straight. I was an alcoholic and I was twenty-one.

My desire to fight when drunk had reached the point where I was now picking out the biggest blokes and belting them senseless. My mates would join in. I was full of hate and anger, mistrustful of everyone, and yet I wanted to be popular.

My uncles Kevin and Gary and I went back to Newcastle, and Murray went to Sydney to look for work. We had relatives scattered all over Newcastle, and once there I steadied the drinking down a bit. I no longer drank metho and made more of an attempt to stay sober. I lived in a humpy in the scrub behind the dump with two men who had known my father. I had applied for the dole but had not yet received any money. I was collecting copper and brass on the dump with these two men and selling it to the scrap dealer.

Food shopping was usually carried out on the dump. There were all sorts of things to eat there if you knew where to look. On a good day it was possible to find restaurant leftovers, canned food without labels, and vegetables that had been dumped by greengrocers. We got to the stage where we knew what was being dumped at what time, in order to grab what we could before it spoiled. We cooked with the pots and pans we found.

It was not the ideal way to live, and after about six months I left the dump to live with my Aunty Maree and Uncle Dan in Hexham. Maree was my Mum's sister. Uncle Dan had been with the Ninth Division in Cairo, and I remember him getting his suit out and going to march in the Anzac parade. It was the only time of the year he wore a suit, and he was probably the happiest around this time of the year too. If someone got him drunk then he'd talk about the war, but when he was sober he'd never say a word about it. There were about sixteen of us altogether in the house; two other uncles and their families lived there, along with Uncle Jim Coogan Brown. He and I lived in the shed out back and we had great times together.

I started work at a spindling yarn factory in Tomago where two of my uncles from Gulargambone were working. It was fairly light work and I always had plenty of energy to go fishing at night. We nearly always caught enough fish and crabs to feed everyone at home. Best of all, fishing kept me out of trouble. I was drinking less at this stage, spending most of my time working, fishing or babysitting. Often if I wasn't working I'd go down to my cousin Ella's by the old bridge at Hexham, to babysit her three sons while she went into town.

On Saturday nights I went up to Karuah to the country and western weekly dance. I stayed sober for work during the week and drank in moderation on the weekends. Probably the biggest improvement in my life was that I no longer drank methylated spirits. I was kept busy during this time, and there were people around to talk to, to do things with. I spent time socialising with my many uncles who worked up in Maitland in the fields.

On one visit there were about twenty-five of us all there. Mum and her husband had just moved back to Newcastle and they were there as well. This meant that all my relations who were originally living in the Newcastle area before I was taken had now returned. One afternoon day we were all sitting around drinking when the police came to the front door to find someone who could identify a Koori man who had been hit by a car and was in a coma. This man, who I did know, died soon after. The man's wife and daughter came out to thank me for identifying the body. This was the first time I had ever met them, but it was a profound meeting. The daughter's name was Lilly, and she was later to become my wife.

Despite this being a stable time in my life, my auntie's place was becoming quite crowded and I was still very restless, so after a time I left the factory at Tomago and started working at the BHP steel mill. It was hot work, especially while working in the molten steel area. The pay packet each week made it all worthwhile though.

I moved in with my mother and stepfather. Mum had two sons and two daughters by her second husband, and they were living at home too. We got on reasonably well, but I made sure I wasn't around any more than I needed to be. I left for work early each morning and arrived home late each evening. At night I would hang around with workmates. Mum had strict rules about drinking in front of children, so I went out as much as I could and only came home to sleep.

At this time I felt that my mother's new children mattered more to her than my brothers and me. I know that our mother never had that continuous bonding time with us and I made sure it never caused any problems at home, but I really believed she didn't love us as much as her new family. Although we had been reunited, the very thing I had longed for all those years at the Home was not turning out the way that I had imagined. It was as though I was being rejected all over again.

Father figure

Drunk, stoned and in trouble. I had started to associate with some very rough people and was making a name for myself. Fate stepped in, in the form of a new girlfriend. Up until then I had never had a girlfriend, only the occasional fling. Then I met Lilly.

On the weekends I would go up to Taree to see Lilly and we'd go out to dances and to the pub. After a few months I asked her to come and stay with me in Newcastle for a few days. I was still working at BHP at the time, and the first few times she only stayed on the weekends, but then we decided to stay together permanently. We lived at Mum's place until we found a place of our own.

I was drinking heavily and unfortunately Lilly drank a lot as well. I still had a desire to avoid being at home too often, so I would go into town to drink three or four nights a week. The drinking led to fighting and soon escalated into physical violence. We often hit each other, but only when we'd been drinking. I bashed her so badly one night that my mother called the police to come and settle it. My mother didn't say much about my drinking because she was drinking herself. We were both trying to bond and finding it difficult, and grog seemed to break the ice.

The constant cycle of drinking and fighting, followed by severe hangovers, was taking its toll. Neither Lilly nor I wanted to continue the lifestyle we'd fallen into, so we decided to start again. In 1969 we made the move to Brisbane. This was a big step for us both, but we reasoned that if we could get away from bad influences around us then we could break the cycle of drinking and violence.

For a while our new life worked well. Our troubles started again when we made a few friends. At first we'd go for a casual drink on the weekends with others, but before long we were getting drunk every time we went out at night. In no time we were hitting each other again.

I was a jealous type and Lilly was even worse. If I looked at another woman on the street there'd be a fight. If while she was drunk, Lilly caught me looking at an attractive woman on the television, she'd throw something at me. I was no better, always thinking she was attracted to men at her job. I treated her badly.

Brisbane was just not working so we decided to quit our jobs and move down to Sydney. Not long after we arrived in Sydney I had to take Lilly to hospital because she kept feeling sick. To our surprise and happiness, we found out she was pregnant.

Despite the excitement of becoming a father, I couldn't stop drinking. We had set up house in Sydney and both of us quickly found suitable jobs, Lilly working part time. Because of some monumental hangovers, I was missing days at work. Lilly quickly tired of my behaviour. She had a baby coming and I was not in a fit state to look after her or a child. I came home one day and found her gone. She had decided to live with her mother at Taree.

Lilly leaving was a wake-up call. I started to reflect on my life, and I was worried that we had split up when we were about to become parents. I wanted a normal family life and I knew I should stop drinking, but I didn't have the will power, support or skills to help myself. I wanted for myself and our child the sort of life that I had been cheated of: a normal family life. Children needed their parents, I knew that, but I didn't know how to manage my own behaviour and the anger I had inside. I decided to go to Taree and try my hardest to get Lilly to come back.

*

Lilly agreed to come back to me, but didn't want to return to Sydney. We decided to go back to Newcastle to live, and once again we stayed with Mum. Not even two years had passed and we had lived at two different places in Newcastle, in Brisbane, Sydney and then back to where we started in the first place. My desire to keep moving was not only very costly, but was also failing to solve the real reasons for moving around so much. A new place didn't solve the problem of old habits.

Lilly's pregnancy moved towards full term. The night she gave birth I was drunk and ended up sleeping with another woman. I was full of regret but I still kept drinking with my uncles every chance I had. I never told Lilly about my one-night stand. We named our baby boy Richard. All the uncles and aunts came around to have a look at the new arrival, and it seemed that I was as popular as I had ever been. Mum fussed over little Richard every chance she had, and Lilly was never short of helpers to look after him either. It seemed life was looking up.

We had been together for about two years by that time, and now that we had a son together, we thought it'd be a good idea to get married. We weren't religious in any way, so chose to marry in the local courthouse just sixteen days after Richard was born. Our mothers were witnesses to our marriage.

We had a party that night and very soon Lilly and I were both drunk. She went off to sleep and I was at the kitchen table playing cards with my uncles. Later that night she came back out, and when she saw me still playing cards she flew into a rage, throwing her wedding ring down the sink. The very first night of our marriage and we were having problems already.

And so we moved again. My mother-in-law, Margaret, had moved from Taree up to Brisbane and was missing Lilly a lot. Lilly dearly wanted to live near Margaret and I believed that my mother wouldn't miss me, so we decided to move back up to Brisbane. Again, we hoped that this would be a new start. I was twenty-two and my son was eight months old.

Lilly had a fairly bossy streak in her, and I know now that this irritated me because I had had years of being bullied at Kinchela. I hated being told what to do. Back then I thought our problems came about because she was smarter and two years older than me. She nagged me about my drinking, and because she nagged I would get angry and drown the anger in drink. After a while it became normal practice for me to go out at night and to not return until the early hours, but the more that I did this, the more we battled.

About a month before we left Newcastle Lilly fell pregnant with our second child. I was already in the habit of staying out all night and coming home just in time for work in the morning. I was determined not to fight with her, so in order to do that I kept away from home. During her pregnancy, she smashed a full schooner into my forehead one night because I danced with another woman.

Our daughter Vicky was a proud new addition to our family. In our traditional ways, the birthplace determines a person's land. We bury the baby's afterbirth in the ground where they are born. Because Vicky was born in Queensland and her afterbirth is buried there, she is a Murri.

By the time Richard was one year old, we were both drinking heavily and fighting. I was hitting Lilly regularly, often resulting in a visit from the police. When we were sober we were a normal family. We'd go for a quiet drink at our local pub, the Ship Inn, a couple of times a week. The trouble was we didn't know when to stop and inevitably things would get out of hand.

There were good times mixed with the bad. We'd go down to the river around West End and Kangaroo Point to catch fish, and took walks along the water. Margaret would look after the kids and Lilly and I would get our good gear on and go out to the nightclubs.

The local Aboriginal people used to go down to Musgrave Park for a drink. It was a long time before they'd even have a yarn with me and longer still before they got to know me well. It was hard for me to be accepted because I was from a different place. In time I became friendly with a few of them, one in particular named Terry. He was an ex-fighter. We went to the pub every afternoon and to the dogs for a bet, usually leaving there without enough for cab fare. Gambling was causing a lot of the contention between Lilly and me. I still loved her, but I just couldn't put up with her complaining, and she couldn't put up with my drinking, gambling and violence.

I was losing a lot of money on the horse races, and in an attempt to reduce this, Lilly would come to the races with me to make sure I didn't go through all our money. On more than one occasion I gambled everything we had and then we'd both end up having to walk home. Those nights we'd argue, and she'd make me so angry that I'd hit her.

Our fights were now so bad that they were becoming dangerous. One night her mother had to pull me off her. I had my knees on her arms and I was holding a pillow over her head trying to smother her. I don't know what would've happened if her mother hadn't been there. When I shaved off my beard Lilly laughed so much that I punched her in the face to make her stop. One night she became so enraged that she stabbed me in the chest. She stabbed me in various parts of my body on about four different occasions. Lilly often accused me of cheating on her after Vicky was born. I was often too drunk to remember what I had been doing. At times I would smash holes in the walls and swear at her instead of hitting her. By this stage of our marriage she was afraid of me. I could tell by the look in her eyes.

One afternoon I came home and found her gone. Her mother Margaret said that Lilly had left me to go and live somewhere up north. Margaret said Lilly had had enough of me hitting her, she was afraid of me she and didn't want to live like that any more.

Looking back, I have often thought I should have told Lilly more about that part of my life that I was trying to put behind me.

I had never spoken much about Kinchela to Lilly, but maybe if I had, she would have understood my over-reaction to being told what to do. Instead of talking about it, I kept it to myself.

I was now left with two children. I hadn't realised until it was too late that I still loved Lilly and wanted her back. Richard was about four years old and Vicky was about three when their mother left. They needed her and I needed her too. Margaret was very good to us, minding the two kids while I was at work. I still worked at the same place in the 'Gabba and made good money. I always made sure I had enough money to buy food for the kids and to pay our rent, but everything else I either drank or gambled away. Working so close to the dog track meant that after I'd had a few drinks I had easy access to gambling. I also got into fights quite a bit, as fighting for me was one way of releasing tension.

I stayed in Brisbane, working and still waiting for Lilly to return. When she first left I really believed she would come back. After all, her children were still there and surely she would be missing them. I was wrong. Lilly never returned, but for months I waited for her, hoping at least for a phone call. Lilly and I had been together for about six years and in that time the love she felt for me had turned into fear. After she left I found my thoughts were increasingly turning to Kinchela and I was increasingly becoming full of anger. I had no real friends to talk to; the only reason I went to work was to keep boredom away.

The kids and I were missing Lilly desperately, but we were all to be left disappointed. She wasn't returning, so about six months after she left I made up my mind to pack up our things and move back to Newcastle. Lilly's mother tried her hardest to get me to change my mind. Margaret was upset when Lilly and I broke up and she still missed her daughter very much. Now I was going to take her grandchildren away from her as well. She had been such a big help looking after the kids while I was at work and on plenty of other occasions as well. She would miss her grandchildren, but I had to do what was best for my family and now there was no reason not to go back to Newcastle. I had to try and build a new life for the kids and me, away from the endless sadness Brisbane had become.

I had no idea what lay ahead, but I had to move on. Now that the train was rattling on down the tracks towards Newcastle, I was sure I was doing the right thing for my children and myself. As we travelled along, I remembered the good parts of our married life together, and leaving Brisbane confirmed that those times were gone forever. Feelings of extreme loss and sadness took hold of me. It was as if the separation had now officially taken place, and from here on I could begin to consider Lilly just a memory of times past.

My two children sat beside me. From time to time they'd ask when their mother was coming back, a question I had once asked a long time ago. It felt like history repeating itself.

Crowded house

A typical Newcastle day: overcast and haze in the air. No-one met us at the station because no-one knew we were coming. The kids and I walked slowly towards my mother's house.

She hadn't had much contact with Vicky and Richard because we'd moved around so much, so now she hugged them so much they started to cry. She looked behind me and asked where Lilly was. I filled her in on the details. It went without saying that we would be staying at her place; one thing about being Aboriginal, you're never stuck for accommodation. Our people do not turn relatives and friends away in their time of need.

I found work at the Newcastle Gas Company digging trenches and laying gas mains around town. I was drinking heavily and the hangovers caused me to miss work. Often I'd be paid on a Wednesday then go out and get drunk that night, miss work on Thursday and then turn up Friday with a certificate from a doctor living nearby who gave out medical certificates to anybody who asked for them.

My boss had known my father Ike and my Uncle Dan, as he and Dan had served together in the Ninth Division during the war. I believe it was due to these connections that I was able to get away with missing so much work.

During this period Murray, Tony and I were drinking at the Rosebuds in Newcastle. One afternoon a police car started following us when Tony was at the wheel. Straight away he panicked, because he knew it would break Mum's heart if he got into any trouble. I was sitting on the passenger side so I suggested he swap places with me. He didn't hesitate, and within seconds I was the one in the driver's seat. The police car pulled us over. They could smell the grog instantly and I was asked to take a breath test, which I failed hopelessly. They took me with them and charged me with drink-driving. The following month when I had to go to court the magistrate noted that it was my first drink-driving offence and so I only received a small fine, but a conviction was recorded against me. Sometime in the future that little deception would cost me my liberty.

Bringing a good wage home allowed me to help Mum out and also pay the way for the kids and me. Mum used to look after the kids while I went out on the town, and it was on one of these nights out that I first met Susie. She had travelled up from Sydney to visit with my cousin. Susie was only sixteen at the time. Despite the age difference we started going out together.

On one of our first dates, we were outside a hotel in the Broadmeadow where the publican there had barred all Aboriginals from entering. We tried to enter and he told us quite bluntly to fuck off. The next day I asked my cousin Boxy to show me how to make a petrol bomb. After a quick lesson, a hastily assembled cocktail was taken to the hotel and I threw it against the wall of the pub. No-one was hurt and I didn't get caught, but inside I was seething with anger.

I had to fight off a lot of competition for Susie. She was attractive. Her father was French and her mother Aboriginal. I had a couple of punch-ups over her, but in the end I was the one she chose to be with. As we got closer, it seemed right to move in together. For the first ten months we stayed with my Mum, and it was during this time that Susie became pregnant with our first daughter. This was good news, because to me it meant that our relationship was now going to be permanent.

Eventually, Susie and I left Mum's house and moved into a rented house in Wickham. My Uncle Dan moved in with us as Auntie Maree had recently passed away. Later his partner Barbara moved in as well. At different times other relatives stayed, and occasionally the place would get a little crowded.

Uncle Jim lived in the garage out in the backyard, preferring to be away from all the noise. Susie took care to fix up his room so that he would feel like it was his own place. I wanted to make sure he was as happy and contented as possible in his old age. Uncle Jim wasn't so much old in years as he was in mind and body. Over the years methylated spirits (he used to call it the 'White Lady') had taken its toll. He no longer had good health and we had to keep a close eye on him. Despite getting the pension he was often penniless. His friends regularly asked him for money on his pension day and he often wouldn't have enough left for himself. This never reduced his grog consumption, but it did result in his drinking lesser quality drinks than he normally would have. Methylated Spirits was the spirit he abused most.

One morning I went out to give Uncle Jim a plate of curried fish soup (his favourite breakfast and a popular hangover cure) and I found him lying in his bed, dead. I gave him a little shake, but he was stiff and had a grey, vacant look about him. He had died in his sleep sometime through the night. Seeing him lying there on his bed in this small garage gripped me with a deep sadness. I went back inside and called for the police and an ambulance. Soon after they came and took his body away.

A couple of days later I had to go and officially identify the body, and it was only then that it really hit me. This formerly proud and talented man was gone. Only a few would remember his title fight in New Zealand, and now this once famous man was laid out on this metal table with strangers all around him. Uncle Jim was a good man who'd had a hard life, and I felt a heavy loss when he passed away. I was often in his company at Platts Estate before I was taken away. He was one of only two relatives I saw while I was at Kinchela. When I found my family out in Wellington, Jim was there, and it was he who made me feel accepted and welcome. It was Uncle Jim who took me over to see Mum for the first time. He even got me work in the gardens out there. Later on, I lived with him out at Aunty Maree's home, and many times when we went fishing he'd talk about his past life. Then he spent his last days living at my home. His was a difficult funeral to attend and he was one person I really miss.

Also living with us at the time was one of Dad's friends, Charlie Thurden. Charlie had previously been in jail for murder, but was released as he was dying. Another house guest was my relative Ian, from Sydney. I was at work and Susie was at home with Vicky and

Richard, when Ian asked if he could have a bath. He said he hadn't had a bath for ages, because his place only had a shower. Ian's first-bath-for-ages resulted in our house exploding and burning to the ground. The fire brigade and police came but it was too late. By the time I arrived on the scene Susie and the kids were standing on the footpath and beside them stood my cousin with singed hair. Even the garage out the back was burnt to the ground. The fire fighters said a gas leak had ignited when a tap was turned on.

Ian came over and apologised profusely, saying that he hadn't had a bath for two years. I looked at him and exploded in anger.

'You haven't had a bath for two years and when you do, you burn my house down!'

It was illogical and unfair but I needed to take it out on someone.

Unfortunately for Mum, the fire meant she would have five extra people in her house until we could move again. It was about four months after the fire when we heard about a vacant flat just over behind Mum's house.

Susie and I settled into our new place, despite always having relatives in the house. Susie seemed to be coping quite well, even though she missed her family and relatives. Being only seventeen years old meant it was quite a task to be with me as well as look after Vicky, Richard and our newborn daughter, Caitlin. In both the children I had with Susie, the Chinese ancestry on my side came out in our daughters' features.

Then one day, totally unannounced, Lilly showed up. She wanted her children back. Susie and I sat down together and tried to discuss this new problem. Susie was against sending the children back to Lilly, but I thought that perhaps they should be with their mother for a little while. It seemed only fair that they spend time with her, but when the kids found out neither wanted to leave us. At the time Richard had just started primary school and Vicky was still at home with Mum and Susie. It would be difficult for them to adjust to a different type of life, because they were very attached to Susie and their grandma. Now we were suggesting they should go away with a virtual stranger.

I thought of Lilly, by herself in Brisbane. After all, we had a child. With this in mind I decided that Richard and Vicky would go to live with their mother in Brisbane. Susie was angry I was allowing Lilly to take the kids back. Mum backed her up by saying that I was wrong to even think about it, and neither of the two children wanted to leave. Vicky thought we didn't want her and that we mustn't really love her. She was heartbroken that her Dad was letting her be taken away, but I was positive I was doing the right and fair thing. To me it would have been unfair not to give them some time with their mother. It wasn't an easy decision, and it made me feel very sad. I loved my children and I wanted them to be with me. Because of my decision, I was seen as the 'baddie'.

People have asked me how I could have allowed this. It is difficult for most to understand. I know what it was like to be deprived of time with my own mother so I didn't want them to miss out on time with their mother. I didn't want them thinking their mother had rejected them, and have the same feelings about their mother as I had about mine. A person who has been stolen has been prevented from learning proper parenting skills, so we do what we think is best at the time. I did feel terrible about it at the time and I was very confused, guilty and sad.

Another thing that people need to understand is that in the Koori culture in which I was raised it is the mother who is the main carer of children; the father is the provider. Of course he loves his children as well, but the role of the mother as far as kids are concerned is the most important — and so I made the decision to let them go back with Lilly, as painful as it was.

I said goodbye to my kids at the station, and within minutes Vicky and Richard were gone. Gone to start a new life, living with their mother. The decision was hurting already.

While Lilly had been visiting in Newcastle we had actually talked about getting back together again. We even spent a night together, over at my brother's house. I felt guilty for cheating on Susie but it made me realise that I could never leave Susie to take up with Lilly. Luckily Susie never found out about my indiscretion with Lilly.

The loss of my two children was hard to bear, but in my second year with Susie another child was added to our family, a little girl we called Shauna. Life seemed good for us then. I was working and only drinking on weekends. Although I gambled a little, my wages were enough to keep us all well fed and clothed and our bills paid. We'd occasionally go out at night while Mum looked after the girls. On the weekends we fished, went on picnics and played games with our children.

Susie and I never fought the way Lilly and I used to when we were together. It was a new life and we were happy. Back then I thought that we'd be together forever and that she was happy to have Newcastle as her home. She seemed content raising the two girls, visiting her friends and spending time with my Mum. They'd go shopping and do all the things Mums and daughters do. I'd sometimes go out with my brothers or relatives, but for the first time I mainly spent my time in the company of Susie and the two girls. I was starting to feel comfortable with my life.

Rock bottom

I didn't see it coming. I should have seen the signs. At first there were just little hints, and then more and more Susie spoke about how much she was missing her family. One night she said she wouldn't mind moving back to Sydney. I had a good job that paid well and I didn't want to pick up and move again. We had discussed moving down to Redfern after the fire, but at that time she was more than happy to stay in Newcastle.

A few months after Vicky and Richard left, an unsettling atmosphere began to appear in our house and at first I thought it was just my imagination. Susie and I were beginning to fight, which was unusual for us. Disharmony crept up on us slowly. I could see a repetition of the life Lilly and I once shared, only this time I was determined not to lose everyone I loved.

We argued more and more as time passed, and even though I knew the reason, I was holding out for as long as I could. In the end it was useless. If we were to have any sort of life together I had to compromise. I already knew her answer was to move to Redfern, and in the end I reluctantly let her talk me into doing just that. Not for one minute did I like the idea of going back to Sydney, but I wasn't going to lose my family because of it.

As soon as I agreed to move the arguments stopped and she was a happy person again. Life in general improved, and it surprised me, because I wasn't aware just how badly she wanted to leave Newcastle. Moving seemed to be my destiny.

My family weren't really surprised to hear we were moving again. I think Mum knew how unhappy Susie was without her family. Once again children were being taken out of her life. She must have felt worse than I ever realised. First the Welfare Board took her four sons, then Lilly took Vicky and Richard to live with her, and now we were taking Caitlin and Shauna away to Sydney.

In Sydney we stayed with Susie's grandmother at Surry Hills until we could get settled. We put our name down for a commission home, but that was some time away. I was keen to get work as soon as possible and started working at Gladesville as a spray-painter. It was a good job and the wages were reasonable. There was a lot of specialist work carried out there, such as painting the equipment used on satellites and other things like that.

Susie and I had now been together for more than two years and it was in our third year that our relationship began to change. We had a problem and we didn't even realise it until it was too late. We'd still go out together at times, but basically we were leading separate social lives. Most of the time I would go out to one of the nightclubs with her uncles and she would go to another nightclub with her aunts. As time went on we went out together less and less, and we considered it normal for her to go her way and for me to go mine. Strangely enough, when we were at home together we got on fine. We were a little less passionate than we used to be, but that was to be expected after two children and a couple of years of marriage. The major change was the separate outings at night.

Leading such separate lives led to Susie being unfaithful. I never thought for one minute that this would ever be an issue between us, and had absolutely no idea that she had eyes for anyone else. I hadn't been feeling well at that time and so I went to see a doctor. He informed me that I had a certain type of medical condition that proved beyond doubt that she had been unfaithful, and I was crazy with anger. Her refusal to admit her infidelity when I confronted her made me even worse. I felt very hurt and betrayed. I didn't want to, but I ended up hitting her and broke one of her teeth.

Just recounting this reminds me of my own past infidelity, and what a hide I had to expect anything different from Susie. But I did, and that was that.

After what had taken place, it was impossible for us to stay together any longer and even though I still had feelings for her, I had to leave. Once more I was losing a wife and once more I was losing children. There I was again, back at Mum's place with another broken relationship behind me. No wives. No children. Marriages were supposed to last and children were meant to be with their parents who would be there to guide them into their teens and then into adulthood. The more I considered how things were meant to be, the angrier and nastier my thoughts became.

In retrospect I should never have given Lilly my first two children, but I never for one minute thought I would be in the same situation again with Susie. I had failed in my first marriage, but to fail at two relationships caused me to feel robbed and cheated, and once again made me think how unfair life could be. Constantly thinking about my failed relationships made me bitter and angry. At that time I never stopped to think about the fact that some of my choices and behaviour had led to the situations I was in. I was running on my feelings only and my feelings were those of somebody who had missed out. I was a have-not, and blaming everybody else for what was happening. I was just thinking that it wasn't fair.

In a matter of months I was drowning out my pain with drugs, drink, crime and women whom I cared nothing for. Along with others I carried out numerous break-and-enters. In the process we caused senseless damage whenever we saw fit as well as taking off with whatever cash was available. Late at night we walked along the streets and bashed passers-by, taking their money from them. I still had a job out at Broadmeadow spray-painting fridges, and even though it was a good job, my heart just wasn't in it. My job permitted me to pay my way at Mum's house and still have enough money to buy grog. My wages didn't however enable me to buy the amount of drugs I needed to supply the habit I was developing.

Like many others, I soon discovered that if I needed a certain amount of 'yarni' [marijuana] on a regular basis, the cheapest way to maintain supply was to grow it. I began my own cultivation in the hills behind Newcastle and I grew enough to keep myself going as well as selling my surplus in clubs. There was never a shortage of buyers, and demand soon outstripped the quantity I could supply. It seemed the logical step to start sourcing from an outside supplier and then resell it to the customers I was gaining.

Usually payment was in cash, there and then. The more product I had to sell, the more cash I possessed. I learned quickly that non-payers had to be taught a lesson, otherwise my reputation suffered. That lesson was a bashing. One night an angry non-payer tried to kill me by driving his car into me, but a friend pulled me out of the way in time.

Because I was in a serious business, I had to expect there might be serious consequences if I wasn't careful or if I upset the wrong people.

Drug sales were now earning me good money. At last I had enough money to buy the fashionable clothes I wanted to wear and to go to restaurants regularly. I had increased turnover to the point where I no longer needed my regular job. Considering the life I was leading I thought I had outgrown that job anyway.

I couldn't in good conscience stay with Mum any longer. I would never have forgiven myself had I brought violence to her place. At no time did I ever stop to consider that I brought violence to other people's places. My thinking wasn't logical; I was on a rollercoaster ride of illegal activities and abuse of grog and drugs to fill the huge hole in my heart that nothing seemed to be able to fill. My days were a never ending spiral of anger and violence. I was on the road to nowhere and going there fast.

*

I moved around from house to house, as it was the safest way to live. I had made enemies, and having no fixed abode ensured I wouldn't have any surprises while I slept. I moved around from relative to relative, friend to friend, only staying for three or four days at any one place.

In time my income increased due to my indirect involvement with armed robbery. If money was short because of drug crackdowns, we'd easily find out who had stolen what from where, and then, using guns by way of threat, we'd demand a hefty share of the proceeds from the crime. We took it as a kind of payment for allowing them to operate without fear of interruption, and naturally there were never any complaints to the authorities. With large amounts of money I was able to gamble as much as I wanted. Sometimes I lost in one session more than I used to earn in a month as a spray-painter. There were also plenty of occasions where I left the table with more than a month's pay in my pockets.

Around that time I became involved with a married woman who had separated from her husband. When the husband heard about it, he used his criminal connections to put a contract out on my life. He was actually prepared to pay someone to kill me, just because I had taken up with his soon to be ex-wife.

I had to make some extreme changes. The first thing I did was to stop seeing his ex-wife, at least until things had settled down some. I had to change the way I carried out all my activities. I was in a position where I couldn't be seen anywhere on a regular basis, because the quickest way to have the contract carried out was to use predictable patterns. No longer could I frequent the nightclubs and conduct my normal business there. I couldn't go to any of my usual haunts, and most importantly I had to keep away from Mum's house. In fact I kept away from all relatives and friends who were known to be close to me. I couldn't risk danger to my family.

After a while, looking over my shoulder and changing my every action daily became intolerable. After about a month I mentioned my dilemma to my cousin Boxy. Because of the clout he commanded within the criminal community, I was sure he'd be able to help me. He'd known about the contract, but was patiently waiting for me to surface to see if I wanted his assistance. This was no time to be a hero. The contract was ruining my business, not to mention my private life. I was more than happy for him to see what he could do for me.

Not even a day passed before the contract was lifted. I don't know what was said to whom, but Boxy had spoken to the right people. I was once again free to move around as I chose. At first I did this carefully; someone telling me that everything was okay didn't automatically mean it was so. Even Boxy could be wrong, and it was my life that was at stake. After a few days I settled down into my normal routine, but I had learnt an important lesson. It seemed the more power you had, the more respect you commanded.

Because my life consisted of unlawful conduct daily, it was only to be expected that occasionally I would get caught. And due to the nature of my crimes, I could also expect to draw harsh penalties. Early on in my career of wrongdoing, I'd receive fines, but it didn't take the magistrates long to learn that I was what they referred to as a career criminal. I found myself in jail on three or four occasions, doing stints of about six to nine months at a time. In 1979 I was jailed for three years.

After spending time in Kinchela, jail was a walk in the park. I ate regular meals, never had to think about where I was going to sleep at night, had plenty of acquaintances in there with me, and didn't have to worry about police chasing me around town. But it wasn't all good. There was rape and violence, so having friends like Charlie Thurden and my cousin Boxy helped me stay out of trouble with other prisoners.

I was surprised at just how many inmates knew me from my activities on the outside. It figured that if so many inmates knew of me, then so did the police. After each release I tried harder to maintain security and discretion in my illicit dealings. Whenever I was in jail I did my time quietly and was released without fuss. Boxy had long ago taught me that there was no point in fighting the prison system, because you can't possibly win.

*

The fact that Susie did not come to see if we could try again stirred up intense anger inside me. I'd heard she'd had a baby. I knew it was the result of her infidelity when we were together. I was told that the father was living in Redfern, and so when I was released I decided to go down and pay him a visit. Accompanied by two mates and two double-barrelled shotguns under the seat of the car, I travelled down to Redfern.

We pulled up in front of a house. There was a man sitting on the front steps.

'Is there a fella called Andrew living here?' I asked.

The man looked us up and down and said, 'Hang on a minute. I'll go get him.' He went inside the house while we waited. Minutes past, but no-one came out, so we went to find him only to be told that the man we had spoken to was Andrew. He had casually walked inside and then ran. I never saw him again. We looked around for him, but in the end it was a wasted trip. I went back to Newcastle, humiliated.

Drugs, grog, gambling and women kept my reputation up, but inside I was crying out because I felt like no-one really cared. My mates were not the sort of people that I could discuss my deepest insecurities or problems with, because men just weren't supposed to do that 'touchy-feely' stuff. Even the day-to-day, simple problems like sickness had to be played down. I didn't want the others to think I was a softie. I had to keep up my image of a tough nut that could handle anything. There was no longer anyone who really cared about my wellbeing and I needed someone to do that. Just knowing there was someone who thought I was wonderful tended to have a very healing, calming effect.

My solution to these feelings was to drown them in a never-ending sea of grog and drugs. I was surrounded by people, was popular and had a reputation others envied. And yet I was the saddest, loneliest man on the planet.

FINDING A WAY

Bad trips and new destinations

Down from the ceiling and down the walls, the monkey-like creatures came. They crawled out of corners and slithered down the walls, chattering loudly. About thirty centimetres long, they had yellowish skin, with demonic, beady eyes and short tails. I was starting to feel hot and I saw my skin was turning yellow. The room was spinning. With both eyes opened wide in fright, I followed them as they came closer and closer to me. Now I was freezing, hugging my bare arms, shaking. Santana was blasting away on the record player. The monkeys were getting closer. Sweating again. Terrified. Hot. Cold. Hot. Cold. They were grinning at me but nothing was funny. Sarcastic smiles on their ugly faces grew larger and larger. Very hot now. And very cold. Help me.

It was about three o'clock in the early hours of a Saturday morning. I had been out all night smoking, drinking, partying on and selling drugs, only this time I had taken some LSD. I was feeling very tired as well as high, so my cousin Gilbert and I went back to Mum's house to sleep it off. I got into bed but couldn't get off to sleep. I removed my shirt and lay there listening. Gilbert was in the same room as me, but he had quickly dropped off into a noisy sleep.

I turned the music off, but it was still screeching loudly in my ears. I pulled the plug out of the wall. I could still hear the music as loud as ever. My mind was racing. I knew I was in trouble. I called to Gilbert, but he was in a deep sleep. I had five brothers and two sisters in the other rooms and my first thought was to go and wake them. But then I thought that because I was the eldest and they always looked to me as the strong one, I couldn't very well call out for them to help me. I then had the idea of going to see my Mum and Steve in their room. But I couldn't do that either, because they'd just think I was drunk again. I called to Gilbert once again. Nothing. By now I was scared and shivering. I lay there whimpering for what seemed like hours.

In my drug-induced psychosis, I thought about my grandmother, Granny Doris. She was a beautiful person, and I remember her saying once how she'd go up into the bush and read her bible and she'd see visions of the Lord in the sky. Well, I was seeing visions now and they were anything but comforting. Then I remembered the bible my first boss gave to me as a Christmas present, when I was eighteen. He used to ask me to go to church all the time, but I wouldn't go. I'd kept that bible in the drawer beside my bed, and right then it was the most important thing in the world. I reached into the bottom drawer for it and placed it on my chest.

The monkey-like creatures were getting closer and closer, my skin was getting very yellow and I was now really terrified. With the bible held tightly to my chest I cried out for my grandmother to help me. Nothing happened. I remembered that my grandmother possessed a very strong faith and thought maybe I should give that a try.

Holding the bible as tightly as I could, I screamed out for Jesus to help me. In a split second, the room was back to normal. The little monkey-like animals were gone and my skin returned to its normal colour. I felt a sense of ease, like a heavy weight had been removed from my shoulders. The room was so quiet and when I lifted my hands into the air it was as if I could touch the stillness, it was so beautiful.

My spirit had been spoken to, and I believe it happened because I had asked for help. I sat for four hours talking with God about all sorts of things, about Uncle Jim and how good he had been to me, and how sad I felt when I found him dead in the garage. Then for the first time in many years I began to cry. I started reading from the bible, I mean really reading it. Not like in the boys' home, where we pretended to read it so we wouldn't get a belting.

Everything that happened to me that night seemed to take only minutes, but while I was reading I heard voices downstairs. It was morning already and I hadn't even realised that so many hours had passed. I felt like I'd had a really long, sound sleep, whereas in reality I'd had none. Something good had happened and I wanted to rush downstairs and tell Mum, but something inside me told me to wait.

That night was the beginning of the end of my three addictions: drugs, drinking and gambling. In one split second, these three things that had devastated my life were taken away from me. There would be many lapses in the future, but this was a turning point in my battle with my addictions. I felt like my life had been taken to the cleaners.

When I went downstairs, my brother Tony was sitting there while Mum made breakfast. He was the one who had given me the acid, the night before. Mum asked me for a smoke. Don't smoke any more, I said. Given it up. They both looked at me in bewilderment, knowing that I used to smoke like a chimney. I offered her $5 to go and buy some for herself.

Smiling, they asked me about my quitting smoking. At first I just said that I had decided to give it up. Then I changed my mind and hurriedly said, 'I've given it up because God took it away from me last night.'

Then I went upstairs. I heard them talking behind me. Mum said to Tony, 'What are you doin' taking Billy out, giving him drugs and sending him all silly?' Tony replied that I was tripping out and that I'd be right in a couple of hours. It was then that I realised why I had been advised not to say anything too soon.

A few days later and even after a week, I was still talking about my experience that night and still not smoking or drinking. Tony kept saying, 'Wow, what a trip... he's still on it!'

After about ten days of feeling happy and telling everyone about my experience, I started to slide back into my old ways. There was too much of my old life around me and not enough reinforcement for my new convictions. A month later, on the way home after a night out, my cousin Gilbert and I saw a wine bar with all the doors open and no-one in sight. We went in and took off with a couple of cases of whiskey from behind the counter. We took them home and then decided to go back to see if we could get more. Altogether we walked off with thirty cases of spirits and wine. Harry, Gilbert and I sat on the bed drinking our spoils when there was a knock on the door. I just knew by the knock it was the police. We looked at each other for a split second wondering what to do. Without thinking it through, I stood up, ran over and jumped out through the second-floor window, landing heavily on the pathway below. I stood up and then started running and kept running until I got to my uncle's place. I stayed there for the rest of the night waiting for things to cool down a little.

The next morning I decided I'd better go over to see how the others got on, but when I tried to stand I couldn't put any weight on my feet. Both feet were really sore and it was a good three hours before I could even stand up. I could barely walk, and had to get my uncle and a cousin to help me over to Mum's place. Mum said Harry and Gilbert had been charged and would be taken to Maitland Jail on remand, while the police looked for another man who had fled the scene. Time to move again. And quickly.

In more pain than I felt I deserved, I caught the train to Sydney. I decided the safest place to stay was at Newtown with some drug addict friends I had there. The pain in my feet was so debilitating that later on in the day I went to the hospital where they were X-rayed. The doctor said my bones were intact, but apparently when I landed on the cement the impact caused the bottoms of my feet to bruise, congealing blood under the soles of both feet. Nothing could be done and it was just a case of waiting for them to heal.

On Friday and Saturday I was left to babysit my friend's kids, because the parents were off on a drug binge. They were supposed to return Friday afternoon with food, but they didn't and by Saturday night the kids and I were starving. The next morning, my friends came back without food, and my cousin Gilbert came over. He and Uncle Shane were off to church and he laughingly asked if I wanted to go. I jumped at the chance, not because I wanted to go to church, but because I knew I would be able to get some food there. This was about five weeks after my encounter with the monkey creatures, and because of that night I was no longer afraid of the church. Even though I had slipped, my belief was still strong.

That first time I went to church I wore a pair of very tight jeans, with a leather jacket and a studded belt. I sat right down in the front row, to show I wasn't frightened. It was the United Pentecostal Church at Mount Druitt.

The service started and people were all raising their hands and singing loudly. I started reading some of the words on the whiteboard out the front and I immediately felt like those words were being directed at me. I was being spoken to, just like the night of the acid trip. Tears started streaming down my face and as soon as the song had finished, I walked forward toward the altar, knelt down on my hands and knees and started to cry. I kept going to that church for Sunday services and the Wednesday night prayer meetings, and after a couple of months I was baptised in winter in a bath full of hot water ready in the backyard with friends looking on. I had been almost expecting a certificate or something like it, but what I received was even more surprising. I began to speak in tongues, in a language that I had never used before, and to this day I can still speak it.

Uncle Shane had a caravan next to the shed in his backyard and he offered to let me live there. My cousin Gilbert was living there as well. He had had been taken to jail for a few days until the case was heard. He was fined for receiving because it was thought he wasn't directly involved in the theft of the grog.

I started going to church with Gilbert who was by now a regular there, mainly to find out what was going on with him. At first I thought he must've had a girlfriend who went to church, but no, he said he didn't.

In time I became a youth leader, and I felt that at last I truly belonged somewhere. No-one knew of my past at that time and I now know it wouldn't have mattered anyway. Now I was well and truly on a straight path. I was finished with smoking, drugs and drinking, and no longer gambled or messed around with women.

As well as attending services at Mount Druitt church, I enjoyed going to other church services as well. Quite often friends I made at these other churches would start attending my church. I didn't ask them to come to our church; they'd just turn up. However, the other ministers didn't like their members being poached and I was asked to stay in the one church. This really hurt me, because I liked going to the different churches around the place, and I thought it was an unchristian attitude.

I was still a member of the Mount Druitt church when I heard about a minister in Redfern who worked with homeless Aboriginals. His name was Dick Blair. This man holds an important place in my life, having been an influence and an inspiration. He held Sunday services in a converted building called the 'Black Theatre'. I went in there one Sunday and was quite impressed with what he had to say. It wasn't long before I was going in there as often as I could to help the homeless, drug addicts, alcoholics and other Aboriginals who used to go there for food and shelter. It worked as an open house where they were always welcome.

The destitute could often be found in parks in the area, and we offered assistance to anyone in need. Those who wanted could come back to our building and be given a meal and somewhere to stay. Occasionally I would take a few of the Kooris from Redfern out to the church at Mount Druitt, just for a change, to get them away from their boring situation.

After more than a year of travelling from Five Dock to Mount Druitt church two or three times a week, I decided to try and get a house out in the Mount Druitt area. Blacktown was only a short distance from Mount Druitt, and I was fortunate to get a house there and a job spray-painting.

Some of the people in the congregation had noticed I never had a female companion. They had concerns about me being so strong in my convictions that I was ignoring my personal life. I know now that I was quite extreme when I first became a Christian. One night at a prayer meeting everyone decided to pray for my first wife Lilly and me. I wasn't interested in resuming a relationship with Lilly or with anybody else at that time.

And then, after five years, there she was again with Richard and Vicky in tow. She had come down to Sydney to see if we could try again. I didn't want to try again. I wanted a simple life. Now, I felt obligated to try and reconcile with her, if only for Richard and Vicky's sake. With the children returning I was forced to make a few changes.

My new faith caused problems between us right from the start. I insisted that no-one drank grog or smoked in our house. When she first returned, I slept on the couch. She was very offended initially, but I suppose she thought in time I would change my mind and things would return to the way they were. My sleeping on the couch worked fine until we had a visitor staying for the night who needed to sleep there. I had little choice but to sleep in the bed with Lilly.

I was only in the bed for about an hour before I realised I wasn't as strong as I thought. After all this time with no physical contact with a woman, it was just impossible to ignore Lilly lying beside me. So many thoughts of the past came flooding back, but instead of being fond memories, I was reminded of our fighting and especially my behaviour towards her. This made me want to make it all up to her by being as attentive as I could be while we were together.

As soon as I awoke next morning, I felt bad about the night before. Lilly knew something wasn't right with me, but wasn't sure what it was. I didn't try to discuss it with her, because I knew she wouldn't understand. I felt no grudge toward Lilly, but I was overcome with guilt because I had no feelings for her and yet I had slept with her: shades of old behaviour.

Lilly and I continued living together with mixed emotions and results. She was full of complaints. She wanted a television. She wanted to go to nightclubs. She was bored with my new lifestyle. I made it quite plain that this was the type of life I led and if she wanted to be a part of it, then she'd have to compromise.

It clearly wasn't working and so after four months she decided to leave, and once again she left Vicky and Richard behind. She moved back to Taree and I didn't try to stop her. I had changed far too much for us to stay together as a couple.

Having Richard and Vicky living with me wasn't such a good idea, because I did not have the time to look after them properly, so three weeks after Lilly's departure I took the children back to her at Taree. She wasn't at all happy when I turned up on her doorstep with two children in tow.

This may seem terrible, returning the kids after three weeks back to Taree. I can say here that this was one of the worst mistakes I made and one of my biggest regrets. At the time I was very extreme in my new faith, I was young, and the pastor of my church advised me to do it. It was bad advice and I followed it, and to be truthful, at that time I was thinking more of myself than the children. The children were affected adversely by that wrong decision in various ways. When speaking about this incident I get stirred up to this day, but my extreme views in those days made me make poor decisions.

Tony, who was with me when I handed the children over, could see that I was upset by the fiery exchange with Lilly, so he suggested we go to one of the old pubs we used to frequent years earlier. I agreed to go to the pub, for old times' sake.

It felt really strange to be entering a hotel once again. We went to the bar and sat down, and then quite out of character I ordered a large ouzo and Coke. I wanted people to think I was only drinking Coke and not grog. Shortly after we arrived Tony left me there and went out to Purfleet to see his people. I should have gone with him, but he didn't suggest it so I stayed at the pub. I sat staring at my drink standing on the bar, then after a while I took my first sip. The next and the next were easier.

I was walking around with my nearly empty glass when I saw Tony arrive back at the bar. He walked towards me with a glass of what looked like lemonade. We looked at each other and smiled.

'What have you got?' he asked.

'Coke,' I said. 'With ouzo,' I added.

'What have you got?' I asked.

'Lemonade,' he said. 'With vodka.'

We both laughed at ourselves and, shrugging our shoulders, knocked back our drinks. After the first glass it seemed easy to have a second, then a third, and that was the start. We ended up staying on a drinking binge in Taree for two days, stumbling around in a grog-fuelled haze. Then, after sobering up enough to drive, we returned to Sydney feeling very guilty and very hung over.

Only weeks after this, my cousins Harry and Gilbert moved from Uncle Shane's at Five Dock to live with me at Blacktown. We got on well together and began to hold prayer meetings at our house through the week. I was asked to stop doing this because attendances at the church were starting to fall. I agreed to stop having the meetings. The people who'd been coming to my house were disappointed, but there was nothing to be done about it. Harry, Gilbert and I seemed to be reasonably popular with the other members of the church and we socialised with them quite a bit.

I did go into a pub again with Gilbert, but this time I left after two beers. As we got into the car, a girl called Phoebe climbed into the back seat and asked where we were going. Home, I replied. She asked if she could come along, and although I didn't really ask why, I said she could. By the time we arrived home Phoebe had gone to sleep so I carried her inside and put her to bed in my room. In the morning I made her a cup of tea and took her to Blacktown.

Phoebe started coming to church with me. I usually drove her home after church, and it was on one of these occasions that we started a relationship.

I took Phoebe to Newcastle to meet my relations. On our first day there we had a few drinks. I really didn't want to start up drinking again, but unfortunately Phoebe really enjoyed getting drunk and was not interested in changing her behaviour. On our last day there, during an argument about her drinking, I got so angry and frustrated that I belted her hard on the leg. It didn't break, but because her other leg was weakened from polio, she was now immobile.

I took her back to my place at Blacktown, and because she couldn't walk I had to carry her when she needed to move. I carried her to the bed, the toilet, the bath. I cooked for her and brought her meals. I was waiting on her hand and foot. When her leg healed we went our separate ways despite the fact that I loved her. I knew that even though I loved her we had too many differences at the time to really make the relationship work. I felt terribly guilty about what I had done. I had thought those days of violence were well and truly behind me.

Bill who?

Everything was now the way I thought it should be: a simple, uncomplicated life. But not for long. Just when I was gearing myself up for the new simple, uncomplicated life, Phoebe came back into it. Pregnant. I was about to be a father once more.

I didn't want to marry Phoebe and she didn't want to marry me as we knew it would not work out even though we really loved each other. I didn't know what to do. I talked it over with my minister and he suggested that the best thing for all concerned was for me to go away for a while. Arrangements were made for me to leave for Brisbane as soon as possible.

The next day I left my home in Blacktown for the last time. My home, my job and my way of life were all gone, because of my stupidity. I left Sydney on the bus headed for a new life in Brisbane.

On a wet Wednesday night, as I crossed a busy four-lane main thoroughfare on my way to choir practice at Mount Gravatt, I was struck by a car. I woke up in the Princess Alexandra Hospital three days later, remembering very little about the actual collision. A nurse was taking stitches out of my eyelid, and in total confusion I asked her what she was doing. She told me I'd been in an accident.

When she had finished I stood up and tried to walk. Every step was agony. I almost fainted with the pain, but I walked slowly to the mirror and saw that my eyes were bruised and swollen. My head was totally bald and had been stitched; there was gravel rash all over it. My right cheek had no skin, and the remainder of my face was all bruised and blown up. I had missing teeth and cut lips and my tongue felt about three sizes too big for my mouth. I looked at my reflection and cringed. Lifting my coat, I saw strapped ribs with skin missing right down one side of my torso. I had severe gravel rash on both legs and other parts of my body. I looked like I'd been through a cement mixer.

I couldn't remember my name and had absolutely no memory of the previous events. Apparently I'd been hit by a car and then dragged along underneath until it stopped. I had skull damage and had been operated on. I now had a plate in my head. I'd been in a coma for three days. I was told I'd just have to wait and with time I'd get better. The doctors were confident my memory would return as the swelling in my head reduced.

The days dragged by and I was getting restless. I was to be kept in hospital until I knew who I was and where I lived. As my wounds healed I moved around the hospital with the nurses accompanying me. I tried to remember my past, but I just couldn't, and as time passed it became more and more frustrating.

Memories were flashing in my head but none of them made sense and I couldn't put the images together. As the days wore on I was having more jumbled recollections, and I thought if I could just get out, I'd be able to fit all the pieces together, so after three weeks in hospital I planned my escape for the next afternoon.

At mid-afternoon the next day I left my room, walked casually down to the front door and then ran out through the front gate. I jumped into a taxi waiting at the rank outside.

I told the driver to just drive. As we travelled through Woolloongabba, I was having flickers of recognition. We headed toward East Brisbane and my memory stirred. The cab pulled up at some lights and as I looked at the bus stop beside us, I remembered. Lilly's house was nearby. I walked up, knocked on the door and waited, all the while hoping I was at the right house. Lilly didn't recognise me at first because of my injuries.

I asked her what my full name was. She thought I was joking at first. She told me my name and then answered most of the questions I asked as well. She told me that the last time I had seen her was when I was living somewhere near Kangaroo Point. I asked her more about my life, but she didn't know much. Apparently we hadn't been in contact more than once since I'd returned to Brisbane.

About an hour later the police pulled up outside and ordered me back to hospital. I told him if they took me back, I'd run away again. Lilly explained the situation as she understood it and the policeman then went back out to his car and got on the radio. After a few minutes he came back and said that it was all right for me to stay there, provided my wife didn't mind. At the time she was living with another man but as I was still her husband and needed her help, she said I could stay. The policeman said I had to go to hospital for follow-up treatment twice a week and then he left.

Not long after Richard and Vicky came home from school. Both looked at me in inquisitively and Lilly had to tell them who I was. They didn't recognise me at first, because my face still had plaster patches on it and I had no hair. I could remember who they were when I saw them, but I couldn't really work out how they fitted into my life. As the evening wore on they became less and less inhibited around me. Lilly had to also explain my presence to her new partner. He seemed friendly, but it was obvious he was a little uneasy with my presence.

My memory was in tatters. Lilly and her partner were smokers and soon I was smoking too, having totally forgotten I had given up. I stayed with Lilly, trying impatiently to fill in the blanks. Lilly tried to help me fill in missing information but what she did tell me didn't seem to fit anywhere in my memory.

Two months later I was watching television and a song came on called 'One Day at a Time'. Hearing that song unlocked my memories. I was remembering my past. Remembering that I was a Christian and that I lived nearby. As the song continued, I cried and was happy at the same time. It is the strangest experience not to know anything about yourself and then for it to suddenly come back. While the song continued more memories came swirling into my brain. I was crying as I ran out of the house, running towards the hostel where I had lived before the accident. I hadn't realised it, but Lilly's house was only one suburb away. I had been there four months.

Another month had passed before I was able to leave. I had been away from Sydney for eight months. The first thing I did on arriving in Sydney was to go and see Dick Blair who put me in touch with Minister Knowles, who let me live in a caravan on his property. By now my memory was totally restored.

*

One morning Phoebe arrived to show me the baby I had fathered. I was living in Redfern at the time and she'd heard I was spending time out at Mount Druitt. She wanted to know what I intended doing about the baby, but I had no idea what I should do. While I was deciding, she got involved with another man and the question of 'what to do' seemed to be taken out of my hands. This man wanted to raise the baby as his and didn't want me in the picture at all.

Phoebe decided to come out to church at Mount Druitt on a regular basis. This put me in a very awkward position, so I thought it would be better if I stayed away for a while. Returning to Redfern seemed to be the best option. I rented a flat and worked as a labourer, staying away for two months. When I did go back it was suggested that I not attend church any more because I was a bad influence on the others. I'd slipped up with grog and had fathered a baby to a woman I cared nothing for. I was shocked that I had to leave over what were human failings, mistakes that anyone could make.

I moved from my flat into one of the rooms above the Black Theatre where Dick Blair held his open-house church. I got a job spraying kangaroo hides down at Botany.

On Sundays it was my job to set the tables and the chairs out and to make sure there was always enough tea and biscuits for everyone. We sang hymns to the accompaniment of two guitars. A few members of the congregation would bring a plate. Some couldn't afford that, but there always seemed to be enough food. After the service it was my responsibility to do the dishes and put away the tables and chairs ready for next time. There was a close community feel at these meetings.

I still had my Falcon back then, so I was able to drive those people who needed food vouchers over to the appropriate charity. Because our church was very poor we weren't in a position to help them with vouchers ourselves. The best we could do was to give out the occasional sandwich and hot meal (just as we do today). We were able to help out in other ways though. There was always someone on the move from one place to another, so we'd help to move their furniture. Moving house was probably what we were called on to help with the most, because Redfern is such a transient society. For three months I did the late night segment for Radio Redfern, staying till three in the morning playing music of my choice. It was a great experience and a lot of fun.

We ended up moving from the Black Theatre to an old convent, just around the corner next to the medical centre. I moved out of my room and into the nuns' old living quarters. After they had moved out, the convent was used as an unofficial drinking place. It was a terrible mess: broken bottles, needles, paper, cartons, human faeces and all manner of things left there. The worst job was the toilets. They were filled to the brim with broken bottles, rubbish and faeces. I had to reach in right up to my shoulder to get the glass and the other rubbish out, before there was any chance of them working. It was an awful job but I was prepared to do it, because Dick Blair's small establishment gave help to many who would otherwise have nowhere to go for support. I felt it was part of my duty.

Money was desperately needed to carry out the renovations. And we received a few donations. During this time my brother David had just been released from jail after quite a long stay, and I was eager to spend some time with him so I made the trip to Newcastle. While I was up there I asked him to come back to Sydney with me, to help me work on the old convent. He said he'd think about it and two weeks later he showed up.

It was during this stay in Sydney that David became a Christian. When it was time for him to go back to Newcastle I asked him to think about moving to Sydney permanently. I couldn't talk him into moving, but he said he'd come back as soon as he could to help. He thought he might come down the following week, but I wasn't to hold him to it. Three weeks later he did come back to help, and now, twenty years later, he's still in Redfern, working with Dick Blair.

My other brothers Murray and Lenny came for a visit. Tony, Harry and Gilbert were also with them. They suggested going to the pub but I wasn't enthusiastic about going. I eventually agreed to go, but insisted on drinking only soft drink. I stood there for about two hours drinking lemon squash while they happily drank their beers.

As time was getting on I said to the group that I had to get back. They ganged up on me a bit, saying I had to have a beer before I left. After asking me three or four times, I told them that I didn't drink grog anymore. However that didn't wash, because I had had a few beers with Tony up in Taree. I agreed to have one and no more than one. But one turned into two and then three and before long I was feeling light-headed. I hadn't had a beer for such a long time, and I think it only took three to get me into that state. Now I was determined to stop, and despite their good-natured protestations I said goodbye to everyone and went to my car.

I was pleased with myself for getting away from the others but that feeling lasted about a minute.

'Blow into the bag, please sir.'

I was over the limit and was told that it would be best if I slept it off. The officer took me inside and put me in a cell where I happily dropped off to sleep. The next morning when I woke up Dick Blair was standing in my cell. Dick was very understanding of the position I had been put in.

I had to appear in court next day. God may have forgiven me, but the magistrate didn't. He sentenced me to six months of weekend detention at Long Bay Jail. On top of that, he fined me $300 and took my licence off me for three years. This was actually my first drink-driving offence, but because I had swapped seats with Tony back in Newcastle years before, the court understandably thought this was my second offence and so delivered a harsher sentence.

They assigned me to do house painting for six months during the day and to report to the jail on Fridays and stay until sundown Sunday. It was 1982 and each night the prisoners would congregate around the television, watching coverage of the Falklands war.

In jail there was great camaraderie and support between the Aboriginal inmates. The others treated me a little differently; they thought there was something a bit strange about me because I said grace at meal times, prayed and tried to share my faith with other inmates if and whenever an opportunity arose.

I have to say that at the time I was no great shining light. I still had vices in my life that I hadn't been able to shake off, and added to this, I was trying to give up smoking at the time and finding it almost impossible.

I finished my time in jail and life on The Block got back to normal. I was still having the occasional beer, and every now and then I'd go and have a bong with the other Kooris around the street. However, my reasons for doing so had changed. I no longer had the addictions that ruled my life; partaking of grog and dope was a way to get the other men to trust and accept me. I started to do a bit of casual work for the medical centre. Once a week I drove their truck to the Flemington markets to buy fruit and vegetables, so the Kooris had good quality food in their diet at a very affordable cost.

Early that year we left the old convent and moved to another place. It was to be known as the Aboriginal Pentecostal Church of Jesus Christ. Just like everywhere else we had been, this place was in need of an extensive clean up and repairs.

On one of the outside walls I painted a big sign that read 'Jesus Loves You'. This sign can still be seen today in Redfern as people ride past on the train. I wrote it there to let people know that there were good things happening in Eveleigh Street as well as the bad. I wanted that sign to send the message that God was in Redfern just as he was in other places.

Jack of all trades

During this period of my life I also worked with the Crossroads Anglican church to help out Reverend Jack Braeside. My main task there was to cook breakfast for up to thirty homeless people every morning, and after they had eaten a good breakfast a few of them would have a shower and be given a change of clothes. Later on at lunchtime I made hamburgers for those who wanted something to eat. After all the cooking was finished, I washed the dishes and cleaned up the kitchen and the showers and got ready to do it all again the next day.

Many homeless people would miss out on regular food because they spent their welfare cheques on drugs, grog and cigarettes. Even though we knew they weren't being very responsible with their money, we were compelled to assist those in need without judgement. Many parents who were hooked on various vices weren't providing food for their children, so we had to take hampers to different families who needed assistance. Then at the end of each day any leftover food was taken up to the homeless men who gathered outside the Black Theatre. The addicts would congregate down the lane, while the alcoholics mostly gathered under the tree at the top of The Block.

There also seemed to be a genuine need for a house and yard maintenance program for people who were unable to do their own repairs and upkeep. Some of the houses occupied by widows and single women badly needed work carried out. I did some repair work during my time there.

I still visited Newcastle once in a while to see my family. On one of these visits Murray, Tony, David and I decided to go to a nightclub, but when we got to the door the Tongan bouncer allowed the others to enter, but did not allow me. He said I had a rip in my jeans. I didn't argue with him and was prepared to just go home when Tony said he had a spare pair of pants in his car. Murray had taken the car keys inside the club. I told Tony that I had a pinch bar in my car and that we could use it to get into the boot of his car. We went to my car and got my pinch bar. I walked back to the bouncer, intending to check with him again about the pants. He saw me approaching with the steel bar and ran inside. I changed pants and went over to the door to gain entry.

Just as we neared the entrance police cars pulled up.

'That's him, there he is!' the bouncer yelled.

I looked around to see who they were talking about. The police ordered me to get the bar and then they took it and put me into jail. On Monday morning I stood before the magistrate.

'It's coz of me pants,' I told him and I filled him in on the details. I also filled him in on my new path in life.

He told me I was free to go.

Not long after this I returned to Newcastle to stay for twelve months. I was given a job with the Newcastle City Council, building a bridge. It was enjoyable work, but although this took care of my days I still needed to seek out a church for support and friendship.

Over the following months I went from church to church and eventually found a church where I felt very comfortable.

The whole Newcastle environment was different, my work was different and the people I was coming into contact with on a daily basis were unlike those in Redfern. I had been happy in Redfern, but it was a very stressful sort of life. By contrast, life up in Newcastle was more casual and relaxed. Most of the people I mixed with during my twelve months up there were either relations or well known to me. It made a welcome change to be with people who really loved me.

Towards the end of my time in Newcastle just prior to finishing work for the council, two police officers came looking for me. When my boss told me about their visit I asked him what they wanted. He didn't really know, but said it was something to do with my licence. They wanted me to go and see them at the Hamilton police station. I thought my three years suspension must have been up. I was really looking forward to getting my licence back and walked to the police station feeling quite excited.

'I've come 'ere to get me licence back,' I told the sergeant at the front desk.

'And you have come to pay your outstanding $400 fine as well? the sergeant asked. 'We've got a bluey here for you.'

It had happened so long ago that he had to remind me. After thinking for a minute I remembered. It had all came about because of a senseless accident in Parramatta Road, which wasn't my fault. Three cars were involved and I agreed to cover for a man who had had a bit too much to drink by backing him up when he said his wife had been driving. The next morning two policemen came to the door and asked to take a look at my car. They left and I never thought about it again. It must have then gone to court and I was found guilty in my absence and fined. Not knowing I'd been fined meant that I didn't pay it, and so it turned to a warrant. After hearing that, he told me I would have to be taken into custody and locked up in the cells until I could arrange payment of the fine.

The warders were on strike at Maitland Jail at that time, so I was kept in the Newcastle lockup for about eight days. I now had a captive audience and there was no stopping me. I was enthusiastically preaching to the inmates so loudly and for so long that some of them asked to be moved. They did not allow anyone to be moved and told the inmates that they would have to stay there with Brother Bill and put up with it. I did my time and everyone was glad to see me leave. I believe that I did have a positive effect on some of the people there.

It wasn't long after my release that I decided to return to Redfern. I had been away for just over twelve months and I felt it was time to return and continue my work there. I found a place in Eveleigh Street to board where the landlady supplied one meal a day for me. It took no time at all for me to get back into the swing of things with Dick Blair, helping to set up the place for the Koori and white kids attending Sunday school in the morning and the congregation for the general service in the afternoon.

I was back, recharged and ready to go to work.

Rock around The Block

Life's fairly tough on The Block. The expressions on the residents' faces tell it like it is: lives in poverty, lives in despair, lives without much hope. And all in a two-hectare area.

*

The Block has been the hub of urban Aboriginal life since the days of the Great Depression. Many Aboriginal people came to find work at the Eveleigh Railyards and settled in the small community bounded by four streets. Prime Minister Gough Whitlam handed over The Block to the Aboriginal people in 1973.

*

One thing I want to make clear: The Block does not deserve the reputation it has as most people who are permanent residents there are good people. Today Redfern has a very transient population. There are always new faces around, some scared, most penniless, many with an addiction and others who are just plain lonely, all trying to fit into a very small, very harsh environment. Crime is rampant and quite often the people responsible are the visitors who use The Block as a lawless refuge. Some good, honest and decent people live here, and it is only a few that give the majority a bad name, a name it doesn't really deserve.

Some come to Redfern looking for relations, others to satisfy their addiction, and there are also many who come to The Block to hide from problems in other communities, and so move into Redfern, trying for a new start. Often the lack of money makes it impossible for the newcomer to stay permanently, and more often than not, these people need assistance to live from day to

A baptism.

Bill Simon outside his house on The Block, 1989.

day. It's to the churches, welfare outlets, soup kitchens and other benevolent groups that they all turn in their time of need.

Many of the young looking for a better life eventually realise that things are actually worse in Redfern than back in their home towns. Often the newcomer catches up with their relations, but find they're suffering from some sort of addiction and in receipt of welfare themselves. The arrival of an extra mouth to feed puts an even heavier burden on the relative.

It's after the money runs out that they find their way to our door seeking help. We give them a meal and a change of clothes if they need it, but our main function with the visitors is to encourage them to return to their home town. If the person has no money, we buy them a ticket, give them a small amount of travel money and make sure they get on the train or bus home.

It wasn't unusual to find young girls on the street with no money and nowhere to go. These girls were vulnerable targets for prostitution, drugs and crime. We'd often take them to a hostel run by a woman out at Penrith. There, they were fed and sheltered until they could be returned to where they originally came from. There was a never-ending number on the streets using drugs and living rough. We could only help those who asked for it and sadly most of them were (and still are) prepared to put up with whatever The Block throws at them in order to maintain their habit. Day after day the ambulance officers would revive young boys and girls who had overdosed. Addicts often berated these officers for causing a waste of a 'good trip'. One of the first casualties of drug addicts was their diet. Many teenagers were starving because all of their available money was spent on their addiction.

In Redfern deals of all kinds were done daily. If you wanted a VCR, a television or a radio, it was just a matter of putting in your order in the morning and you could usually take possession by that evening.

Just about all of the people on The Block are Kooris, and when it comes to authority or outside interference it is a very close-knit community where strangers are not trusted and usually not welcome.

During this time my cousins had come to stay, with the land-lady's reluctant agreement. One night they came home stoned and proceeded to raid the fridge, making so much noise that they woke the landlady who came downstairs to investigate. An argument followed and one of my cousins hit her, breaking her jaw. By the time I got home from visiting my mother in Newcastle, our landlady had been taken to hospital and the police had taken my cousins away to be charged. I felt terrible about what happened to her, because it was at my request that she let them stay there in the first place. After she was discharged from hospital, things between us were very strained and I decided to leave. She was one of the few white people on the street who had earned respect because she was always kind to Aboriginal people.

My new house was a few doors down, a small brick house on the corner of Eveleigh and Holden streets, owned by a Jewish fella. He and I had many lively discussions about theology, and we got on really well together. The house was looking a little dowdy, so I painted the brick red and the mortar in between I painted white. I then added a bright blue patio so the house stood out rather well. No-one missed it when given directions.

My mornings always started with a broom. Before the day could begin I'd sweep away the broken bottles, garbage, syringes, vomit and whatever else had been deposited overnight. Then I'd pick up the discarded handbags. Thieves would rob women in the streets nearby then return to The Block for sanctuary. Usually they took the money and credit cards and then would throw the handbag away. I'd take the bags up to the police station, so that anything important would be returned to the owner. The local police were used to this procedure and they also knew not to ask me who was responsible. Most of the time I didn't know anyway.

I always made sure there was soup on the stove and I'd buy as much extra food as I could afford to feed the hungry. People respected my beliefs and treated my house with care. Sometimes I would have a cigarette and a beer with the locals. I didn't want them to think that just because of my beliefs that I was better, cleaner or more virtuous than any other person, so having a drink and a smoke was a good way of inviting their trust. Many different families came to my door for help, and my home was known as a welcoming, safe place.

Grocery bills were a never-ending problem. It seemed no matter how much food we had it was never enough. More and more

Bill Simon's Story

Bill Simon's house, with a cross in Aboriginal colours on the balcony, 2008.

Bill Simon ministering on The Block.

people were making their way to our door and we just couldn't keep up with the demand. As well as these people there were those who were lying in the park unable to walk, and they needed food taken over to them so that they wouldn't starve. Fortunately I was able to operate a fortnightly account. Unfortunately it got up near to $1,000 once and the only way I could pay it was by selling my car.

My son Richard came to live with me on The Block for a while and assisted me with helping the community. His sister Vicky kept asking if she could come and live with us too, but I wouldn't allow it, because it wasn't safe for her there. At different times there were all sorts of people sleeping on the floor of our house. It just wasn't the place for a young girl to be unless she was under constant supervision. At the time I had no way of knowing just why it was so important for her to get away from her mother's place. Her mother's boyfriends made her feel unwelcome in her own home, and in the end she blamed me for not rescuing her. I was concerned about Richard living in Redfern and coming into contact with crime, even if only as a witness to the lawlessness, but fortunately he was fairly streetwise, and in no time at all learned to live with this way of life instead of falling victim to it.

As time went on Richard became more and more helpful. He gathered the homeless, helped with feeding and clothing them and was always willing to go to someone in trouble and do whatever he could. Occasionally he'd drink too much and gamble as well, but he was compassionate to those in need and I valued his contribution.

It wasn't all gloom and doom. One of the happier times on The Block was when the protest rally was held in Redfern Park because of the tall ships' arrival in Sydney harbour. Aboriginals came from all over Australia to participate. To Indigenous people, that re-enactment of the tall ships coming to Australia was a reminder of the British invasion. All the Kooris met in Redfern Park and then went down to where the tall ships were docked. Peaceful protestors went to Hyde Park while the more vocal went down to the docks. Loudspeakers had been set up in the park with music and singing filling the air. We all sang and prayed together, and afterwards went back to Redfern, satisfied that our protests had been registered.

Richard and I were living in Eveleigh Street during the uprisings of the early 1990s. The area of Redfern referred to as 'The Block' is considered to be Aboriginal land. With this belief firmly in their minds, the residents of that area reject whitefella law being implemented, and especially reject whitefella interference in the day-to-day activities there. I was there as police kicked in doors of people's homes and people retaliated.

During the riots it was my moral duty not to participate in violence. I stood on my balcony silently praying for all concerned, but Richard was out there in the thick of it, as were most of the other young men. A newspaper reporter asked me for my opinion and I told him the Old Testament story of the fiery furnace as an analogy to what was happening and my role in it. The next day the headlines in the newspaper read, 'Bill Simon says Redfern should be burnt to the ground.' I believe my words were twisted purposely. Nothing like a sensationalist headline to sell papers. I was not impressed.

My personal life was in a mess at this time. I became involved with a woman named Maddie who I believe I could have settled down with. We were compatible and she had the qualities of someone whom I could have made a new life with. She became pregnant to me and had an abortion without my knowing. She tried to justify herself by saying that she knew I'd be against her terminating the pregnancy. She was right too. I was angry and very sad. Because of her decision, I knew that I would never be able to let go of my anger and so we decided to go our separate ways.

Living on The Block sometimes tested my strength, and there were times when I was overwhelmed and lacked the compassion and patience that I should have had. I had been in Melbourne at a convention when my money ran out, so I asked Richard to deposit some into my account, but he hadn't done it. I went into a church to ask if I could have a food voucher and I noticed about a dozen young people standing out the front. Inside there were two long tables covered with various dishes of food for a function. A man was on the phone inside speaking to the police, complaining about the people outside and wanting the police to move them on. All the way back to Sydney I felt sad for those young people standing out the front of that church. They were hungry.

I arrived back at Redfern feeling angry that Richard hadn't put any money into my account when he should have. I walked into my house and there were bodies laying everywhere, snoring away. In anger I yelled out for everyone to wake up and get out. After they had left I sat on my bed crying at the unfairness of life, when it struck me that I was behaving no better than those people in Melbourne who had refused to feed the hungry. I rushed out onto the balcony and called everyone back inside. Then I sent Richard up to the corner store to buy sausages, eggs and a couple of loaves of bread to feed them all. Richard told me later that the CES had stopped their money and they hadn't eaten for days.

Stories from the streets

One morning I was walking up the street in my three-piece suit when I saw a tall thin fella in a long raincoat walking down the street toward me. As he got closer I had a vague feeling of recognition. I remembered back to Kinchela and how I often played tricks on him. Tim walked right up to me, very determinedly, and I reached out and hugged him. Soon we were hugging, chatting and behaving like long-lost friends and I asked him back to my place for a coffee.

Much later our conversation turned to Kinchela. Tim told me that my practical jokes had played on his mind for years. He had been in Sydney when he heard that I was living in Redfern. All the pain and hostilities of Kinchela came flooding back and he was determined to make me pay. He opened his coat and showed me the machete tucked under his belt. He told me that he had intended to kill me but he had changed his mind when I hugged him a few hours before. He now saw me as a fellow Kinchela boy who had suffered the same things he had suffered, and from then on there was an unspoken bond between us.

All respected my home and I never once had to worry about anyone breaking in and stealing. Many times over the years the police have come onto The Block looking for drug dealers and various other lawbreakers. They never once asked to search our house.

Being trusted in Redfern was not always a good thing however. Because many people knew that I would help a fellow Koori in need, they often asked for favours. A friend of a friend once asked me to mind a parcel for him. I agreed, but that same night I had a bad dream about the parcel and I opened up the box. There were two guns inside. About four or five months later he needed a place to stay once again and I gave him shelter, only this time I made sure there were no boxes of any kind.

It didn't occur to me at the time that I may have been harbouring a fugitive and I didn't bother asking details. He got sick after a few months, fell into a coma and died a few weeks later.

Richard often brought home runaways. We'd give them a meal and then send them back home. Once he brought a fella in off the street who had been beaten up and was seriously hurt. We looked after him at home as he refused to go to hospital, and we had no transport as I'd sold my car. When we got up next morning he was dead.

One Saturday afternoon I was walking to the station when I noticed a Koori fella looking drunk walking towards me. This fella had been released from jail and all the locals were well aware of who he was. I had no idea of his reputation. Everyone despised this person as he had been jailed for paedophilia. He was an outcast in prison. He was an outcast in Redfern. When he got close to me he fell down, so I picked him up and helped him into my house. The first thing I noticed was that he had messed himself. I undressed him and wiped up all the faeces, put the bath on and cleaned him up. After his bath I wiped him dry and gave him some of my clothes to wear and threw his clothes in the bin. I offered him some food, which he eagerly ate and then I put him to bed. I found out later that he had come from the pub up the road where the patrons had bashed him with an iron bar.

On my way out next morning I told him to make a sandwich and I'd see him later. The next day he asked if he could come with me to a morning service. The people in the congregation couldn't believe that this fella had turned up in a church. On that day he decided to change his life and ask for forgiveness for the terrible crimes he had committed. After the service I took him back to my place for some lunch.

This man was estranged from his family. It was easy to tell he had made a serious mistake that he extremely regretted. I had an enormous urge to help him. I despise the act of paedophilia as most people do, and in fact I despise it even more because I grew up at Kinchela where boys were subjected to sexual abuse, and I have seen first-hand the terrible consequences of this form of abuse. I have known the responsibility of trying to protect my brothers from it, and as a parent I try to protect my own children. However, I felt my duty was to help this man get back on the right track, as he was willing to change his life. I put him back in touch with his family, who came to take him home. I never saw him again but I live in hope that he was able to start his life over again.

I met a fella sitting in a gutter drinking port who knew my relatives. He finished his port and then he came over and had a meal. He had nowhere to stay so I offered him a bed for the night, which he gratefully accepted. This fella had the reputation of town drunk. His wife of twenty years no longer wanted him, because of his drinking, and you could tell by his voice that he wasn't proud of any of it. The next morning I got ready for church and he decided that he'd like to come with me. I gave him a quick haircut and a shave. He cleaned himself up and I brought him some different clothes to wear. We went off to church and he sat quietly in the back of the congregation listening with interest. He was illiterate but I taught him how to sign his name and a few other paperwork essentials. After he had been with me for about eight weeks, we went to a bank and to Social Security to fix up his paperwork for his pension and so get him established in the area.

In a matter of months he was rounding up drunks in Redfern and talking to them about his new direction and encouraging them to stop drinking. He said he was living proof that it could be done, and he wanted to save as many as he could from the fate he had been heading for. Eventually he was reunited with his wife and family and he had five months of a new life with them before he died from a grog-related illness.

My brother Murray did not understand my need to help my fellow Kooris. Whenever he came to stay with me we always ended up in disagreement. I was trying to encourage people to come to my home when they needed assistance, and he was forever turning them away. He didn't like strangers coming into our home. He wasn't comfortable with drunks and so many 'down and outs' traipsing around the house at all different times of the day and night. He didn't understand that there weren't many places they could go for help and shelter. He made people think twice about coming to the house, and it ended in a punch-up and him returning to Newcastle.

Even though I was doing good community work, I was never an angel or a paragon of virtue. Old habits are hard to break. On occasions I went with prostitutes up at the Cross even though I always felt very guilty about it afterwards. It took me some time to overcome this problem.

Sometimes I would reach the point of burn-out, and the only way to recharge my energies was to take time out from Redfern and visit Newcastle. At times I'd ask myself, 'What's the point of doing all this? Feeding everyone and trying to look after them all the time.' Especially when the next day we'd see them drunk again, stoned again, in trouble again. But on occasions when I would feel despondent, there would be a phone call or message, just at the right time, from someone who had changed their life because of their time with me, and this would make it all worthwhile. One afternoon, when I was feeling a bit low about my work in Redfern, I received a phone call from a fella who had picked me up hitchhiking near Taree. He told me that something I had said to him had made him take a new direction in life and he was ringing to say thank you.

Redfern is full of stories. It is a diverse place, and for me one of the most interesting places in Australia. Yet for the people who live there, boredom and apathy are some of the biggest problems they face. Redfern was (and still is) a sad place, although occasionally some good things have happened there. From time to time important people from all walks of life have come to The Block. Once we had some rap dancers from America come there in big limousines. Cathy Freeman, Cassius Clay and Michael Jackson have been there, and one time a group called the Living Waters came to perform at a tent meeting right there in the park. About three hundred turned up for that. For many, The Block remains a curiosity. Celebrities go there just to see what all the hype is about.

The really important people however are not those that arrive in limousines. The important people are the ones that have been forgotten, whose voices and faces are not seen or heard: the

Men performing on The Block.

dispossessed, the poor, the Stolen Generations, the addicted and homeless. When curiosity becomes generosity these people may have a chance.

Bringing up the past

I'd been in Redfern for ten years and the time came to move on. I was never one to dawdle after I'd made a decision, so within a week of deciding to leave I packed up my few belongings and moved back to Newcastle. I was sad to be going, even though I knew it was the right thing to do and the right time to do it. After so long I wondered what would become of the people who had come to rely on me so much. I'm sure I wasn't irreplaceable, but at the time I wondered whether there would be someone willing to fill the space my leaving created.

I hoped I was embarking on a brand-new, more mature phase of my life. For a while I had to live on Social Security, but I did some handyman work as well. At this time I had plenty of time to spend with my family. Going back home was the right decision. Occasionally I missed my friends in Redfern, but the enormous pressure that was ever-present in Redfern was nonexistent up in Newcastle.

I had a need to reach out to Aboriginal people and was given permission to use the church at Broadmeadow of a Saturday. After a lot of word-of-mouth advertising our first service was packed. Kooris came from all around and felt very comfortable attending a service especially for them. Standing out the front speaking each week was quite draining and it helped a lot going to another service to be recharged. Unfortunately we didn't get the resources we needed to continue, so I changed churches again.

The ministers at the Foursquare church in Toronto had a heart to help Aboriginal people. They took an interest in developing programs to enrich Kooris and I wanted to be involved. It was here that I met Katherine who was to become my wife. Romantic thoughts were just not part of the equation. I had closed the door on that part of my life. She was mistrustful of men and I felt women distracted me from my work, but over a year we became close doing outreach work together, and fifteen months later we married. There was no honeymoon. There just wasn't time. Our first home together was at Gateshead. I still had the desire to help Koori people in my area, and so set up a hall for services on a Sunday for the people around Windale, with some financial support from the Foursquare Church.

It took two years with Katherine before I felt that I could talk about my past. I told her about my brothers' removal and mine from Platts Estate. And then I told her about Kinchela. Not too much at first, but enough so that she understood. I needed her to understand that my time there was the reason that I had problems, many of them that I still struggle with even today. After gradually telling her about my whole past I felt guilty; it all sounded so horrible that I wasn't sure just how she would take it all. I was compelled to be truthful, and I felt as my wife she had a right to know all about me.

Katherine listened attentively as I told her the very private, personal parts of my life, which until then had been shared with no-one. I was confiding much more to her than I had to my previous wives, and retelling some of the information I needed to pass on was quite an emotional experience. Katherine quietly listened to all I had to say and then I waited.

She was with a new person, she said, and what the old Bill had done was no longer relevant.

'It's all in the past,' she simply said.

Katherine was totally supportive of my desire to help my own people. Within a few months Aboriginals from around Belmont, Swansea and Windale were attending our services. Many non-Kooris came as well. We called it the Kooma Christian Church, and slowly we were attracting people from all over the area. People felt at ease in our church, and word got around that this was a place where Kooris could feel comfortable. Community spirit and care grew strong over the months.

As well as the indoor services, we were also holding open-air gatherings at Charlestown and other places. These were very successful and provided the opportunity for those who didn't like the formality of indoor services. Many Aboriginal people prefer to be outdoors when in unfamiliar surroundings. This is so often the case when attending funerals and also at court sittings. The only time they're inside is when it's absolutely necessary, and as soon as possible they prefer gathering around outside.

Even though we were kept busy at Windale and life was fulfilling, Redfern was still in my mind a lot of the time. I still felt very connected to The Block, and every six or seven weeks I went back there to support Dick Blair. My thoughts about assisting my own people were so strong that I wasn't really interested in supporting non-Koori people. I often felt that my attitude was wrong but it still didn't change the way I felt. My belief at that time was that white people already had many resources whereas Kooris were short on everything. The other reason for visiting Sydney was to see my brother David, who was in jail at the time.

After about a year and a half at Windale, we moved to Mayfield, allowing us to upgrade our situation. We now came under the Apostolic church and we were now a fully registered church with all the appropriate backing and validation required by the tax department.

It was while we were at Mayfield that Katherine and I became parents. In 1993 our daughter Sienna was born. Her birth helped to make up for the sense of loss I'd long felt regarding my other children, and it gave me a deeper sense of security within my marriage. This was my last chance to be a good father, and I was determined not to repeat my past mistakes. Over the years I've loved and in some ways lost all of my other children, and this wasn't going to happen again.

It was when Sienna was about two years old that we were to become parents once again. Katherine was pregnant with a baby boy, but our happiness was short lived when about three months into her pregnancy, Katherine miscarried. Our sadness was compounded by the news that due to health reasons Katherine shouldn't ever fall pregnant again. It took quite a few months to reconcile ourselves to this situation. As the years passed Katherine learned much more about Kinchela and was a confidant to quite a few other Kinchela men who still suffer from the traumas they experienced at the Kinchela Boys' Home.

Stories from the cells

How do you remain objective and compassionate when you deal with some of the State's most violent and brutal men — men who have raped, tortured and murdered innocent people? Some would think it difficult, even impossible, to get past the terrible things these men in jails had done, but I knew I had the skills to do it. I have the gift of the gab, which helps. Rob Moore, the Anglican minister at Cessnock, told me that the entire prison population was my congregation and there was no-one there beyond redemption. This has stayed with me for many years and whenever I was with what I thought to be a hopeless case, I reminded myself of what he had said. This man made my new mission, prison work, much easier, and it was only because of his assistance that I was able to function successfully.

The hall we rented as our church at Mayfield had to be abandoned because of contractual problems, so we decided to attend the Apostolic church at Maitland. After a while the distance from our house to the church became impractical, so we rented a house in the small town of Rutherford.

Like all towns, Maitland had its share of underprivileged people. I arranged with two local cake shops to collect their leftover bread and pies so I could deliver them to families without food around Rutherford and Maitland.

Katherine had worked hard since I'd first met her, and now that we had moved to Rutherford with our young daughter, we both felt she should have some time out to be at home with Sienna. While we lived in Rutherford she tried to keep her work outside the home to a minimum, spending her time teaching Sienna the things we wanted her to know.

I have a closer relationship with Sienna than I do with my other children. I suppose that's because our family unit is still intact and also because I'm getting older. This doesn't mean I love my other children any less; it just happens they live away from me and have their own lives as grown-ups. We still keep in contact with each other, spending time together whenever possible.

Living in Rutherford suited us fine and it put me right where I thought I could be the most help. At the time I became interested in the prison ministry. The chaplain at Maitland prison helped me get accredited and approved for prison work. Before approval could be granted certain criteria had to be met, and one of them was to make sure I hadn't been in prison in the previous ten years. Even though I had been incarcerated when I was younger, I had been law-abiding for the last ten-plus years so I was fine. The different checks only took a few weeks, but I was impatient to be accredited so that I could get on with the work.

One thing I had in my favour was that I had been on the other side of the bars in three different jails. This proved invaluable, because I understood the situations that had landed them there and I knew how to speak to these men. Some of them I recognised from my younger days up around Taree and Newcastle. Some of them were related to me and some I knew from the last ten years.

'Brother, what are you doing? You should be in here with us,' one of them exclaimed when he saw me. 'You're on the wrong side of the bars.'

On one occasion I had just finished yarning with an inmate when I looked at my watch to check the time and I noticed it wasn't working. This prisoner said that he might be able to fix it for me. I told him that if he could fix it, he could keep it. I handed him the watch and he thanked me, saying that he'd have no trouble repairing it. I wasn't so sure. By the next visit, he had fixed it so I gave it to him. Little did I know of the trouble I was about to cause.

It wasn't long after that I went to a retreat at Wyong. Because it was a place of reflection and quietness, there were no telephones. We weren't allowed to leave the compound and were allowed no visitors. We were permitted to read our mail and it was at this retreat that I received letters from my daughters, telling me of their love for me and what I meant to them as a father. It was a really wonderful experience reading the compositions of my children's thoughts. That night I slept the sleep of someone totally contented with life.

One of the other participants at the retreat told me that he had visited Maitland prison the day before. He told me about a prisoner who was put through a spot security check where the guards found him with somebody else's watch. They confiscated the watch and then suspended all of his visiting privileges. Because it was the third time he had caused trouble, it had been decided that he should be moved to Long Bay, a higher security prison.

I felt sick when I heard this. I asked permission to make a phone call to the prison and I was reminded that a retreat was where the outside world was not allowed to intrude. I pleaded to make the call and was finally given permission.

I rang the prison and spoke to the warden, who wasn't the least bit moved. He said the prisoners knew only too well about contraband, and anything in their possession that is not listed in the property book is illegal property. Knowing this the inmate was obliged not to take the watch in the first place and as a long-term prisoner he should have known better.

By this time I was feeling really bad. After having three days at a retreat, feeling extremely happy and relaxed, I was now anxious. I couldn't believe that my trying to help someone could have caused so much trouble. The warden wouldn't change his mind, so I just apologised, said goodbye and hung up. I went back to join the others with all previous feelings of exhilaration now a not-so-distant memory. Dark clouds of worry floated around in my head.

Two weeks later when I returned to Maitland Jail I saw the fella who had fixed my watch. I asked him why he was still there, but he didn't know what I was talking about. I reminded him about the watch. The inmate smiled and told me that one of the bullies had taken the watch off him, and now that inmate had been caught and transferred to Long Bay. After I heard this, I smiled too.

Having permission to go into the Maitland correctional facility allowed me to access Cessnock Prison as well. In addition to that I was able to go to Muswellbrook once a month, if the church budget allowed me to do so. This enabled me to provide assistance, companionship and fellowship to the inmates in three large prisons. I wanted to spread the word, as well as give day-to-day outside contact, which the Koori men needed and in most cases welcomed. The prison chaplain wasn't worried which prison I went to, as long as I kept in contact with him and kept him alerted to any problems.

I had a very casual way of getting to know the men in jail and it still works for me today. I usually walk up to a fella and simply introduce myself and ask if he wants to have a chat. More often than not they will be quite happy to have a talk. I never tried to force myself where I wasn't welcome. This casual method was far better than arranging a time and making it an official appointment, because the inmates were always sceptical of anything official. One opening question I often asked was if he had any visitors coming. This allowed the inmate to indicate his circumstances and also showed that I cared about whether he had contact with the outside world. Another important question was to find out if his family on the outside was all right. Often if the breadwinner is incarcerated, the family on the outside do it fairly tough. Many a time the help extended to a prisoner is not extended to his family on the outside. If I knew somebody from the same home town as the inmate I was speaking to, it made it much easier to enter into conversation. His eyes would light up in recognition, and before long we'd be yarning about old friends who were common to us both. It was often very hard to bring a spiritual dimension into the conversations as most inmates had other concerns to think about.

It is politically incorrect to ask him about his crime. He would tell me if he wanted me to know. Frankly it made no difference to the way I treated him anyway. I was aware of his crime beforehand, as I was given a file on each person I dealt with. It was not for me to cast judgement or speculate on his guilt or innocence. Prison work requires this attitude. I also could not let my own emotions overwhelm me, no matter how tragic the situation. In visiting the detention centre at Broadmeadow I had to put this into practice, as I dealt with many teenagers who were incarcerated for very brutal crimes.

After they got to know me, the inmates would start to feel at ease and open up a little more. It required a few visits with friendly conversation before the man's own judgement would make him feel more relaxed in my presence. We'd talk about the things he needed to get off his chest, regardless of the topic. By the time we reached this stage he would usually have told me why he had been incarcerated, and I took that as a sign of his acceptance. I was always cautious not to intrude on his personal life. These men are by nature very distrustful and are unlikely to give any information that may incriminate them further or cause harm to their families. There were some who trusted no-one and rejected all attempts at conversation.

There was a 28-year-old inmate who had hepatitis C. He had made it his habit to spit at any guard who came within distance of him. The guards had to wear a shield to go near his cell and always slid his meals under the door. Even walking past his cell, the guards had to be very careful. I desperately wanted to talk with him because I knew he was hurting. Despite advice not to go near him, I went in and sat down next to the bars of his cell. From the look on his face I could tell straight away that this was one angry young fella.

He knew he was dying and therefore he felt he had nothing to lose, but I think it was because of my audacity that he showed no anger towards me. I sat quietly next to him as we spoke about different topics of no particular significance. He told me a little of his life and I told him a little of my past. Slowly he began to accept me and eventually we talked together with ease. He still wouldn't let the guards near him, but that was none of my business. Over the following visits I began telling him how I had changed my life. Although very doubtful, he listened and as time went on he showed more and more interest in what I was saying. Eventually he decided to follow a spiritual path, and months later, when his time to die came, he accepted his fate and felt much more at ease.

I was visiting the high security remand section of the prison one day when I met a huge Aboriginal man with marks all over his body and a beard down to his chest. He was a kadaija man. In whitefella language that means he was a witch doctor — a feather-foot. He had been jailed for the alleged kidnap of a nine-year-old Aboriginal girl, and when he saw me he thought I was there for some kind of tribal payback. I told him I wasn't there to pass judgement on him, and after a while he settled down and we talked. I knew I would never be able to persuade him to abandon witch doctor beliefs, but just the fact that he was willing to talk was satisfying.

I spent time with Ivan Milat and Kevin Crump during my time in prison work. Both these men are notorious multiple murderers, but I saw a good side to both of them, buried deeply within their damaged psyches.

At one stage I was spending quite a lot of time with Kevin Crump and I asked the congregation at our church to pray for him. They were all in favour of doing as I asked — until I mentioned Kevin Crump's name. Because of the brutality of his crimes, they refused to pray for him. I was shocked hearing this and reminded them that it wasn't our place to judge, but nothing I said would change their minds.

Other places I visited regularly were the Stockton hospital for the developmentally disadvantaged and the Morisset facilities for general public psychiatric patients, the criminally insane and terminally ill patients. We'd push the wheelchair-bound patients around the grounds and clean up those who had messed themselves or vomited. I'd take other volunteers (of which there were few) in to visit with the patients.

One morning while visiting I recognised an ex-Kinchela fella who had been a work boy during my time. He didn't recognise me at first, but after we spoke for a while the memories started coming back. Strangely enough he enjoyed talking about Kinchela, even speaking about sad things that had happened to him there. Kinchela was not a subject he would discuss with others, but because I had been there and shared the same experiences, he felt at ease. He did however keep asking me to get him out of the hospital and to take him home. This was impossible. His mind was damaged and he was never going to survive on the outside.

There was one section of the hospital where I was absolutely no help whatsoever. It was the lock-up section. These were the patients who had no control over the urge to hurt and to kill others, and because of this, they seldom came into contact with other people and never with anyone from outside the facility. They had a small area where they could walk around, but I wasn't allowed anywhere near them, because of their involuntary violent behaviour.

The only person who ever came and helped with fellowship at the hospice and the asylum was my mother's brother, Uncle Gilbert. We'd converse with the patients, and because the hospitals were always short-staffed, we'd help clean up people who had messed themselves and wipe vomit away from patients' faces. This was the same Uncle Gilbert with whom I had sat with on the banks of the river out at Gulargambone drinking methylated spirits. Uncle Gilbert and Uncle Kevin managed to get back on track, leaving their self-destructive ways behind and joining me in a life devoted to our faith.

Each week I'd hold a church service in the jail. Being only one Christian voice among the Koori jail population meant I was unable to spread the word to as many as I'd have liked, so I asked the warden if I could play Christian videos over their entertainment system. I rented the material from local video shops and gave them to the guards to play throughout the week.

To me, my job in the prisons was clear. The inmates were there because they broke the law and were repaying their debt to society, and I was there to provide encouragement, understanding and spiritual help to whoever needed or wanted it. It frustrated and saddened me when I could plainly see someone who desperately needed help, but was unable to accept any assistance. Inmates would hold back their feelings, even when it was not really their wish to do so. This sort of thing happened for various reasons, peer pressure being one of the main ones. Regardless of the successes or failures I had, I wasn't ever discouraged.

Sad to say, out of the seven different churches we had asked to help with the patients at Stockton, Uncle Gilbert's was the only one who didn't hesitate to jump in and do what was needed. It's really a sad fact that so many patients went without spiritual help just because asylums weren't pleasant places for outsiders to be in.

There were so many sad stories in those hospitals that to have any chance of being effective, I had to take care not to get too attached to any particular patient. Visiting was very taxing and I usually returned home totally drained. The patients were often so desperately glad of some company that they unintentionally sapped all the available energy from a visitor. It was by no means their fault and I still found it difficult to maintain a detachment from some of the really sad cases there, especially if I had been seeing them for a quite a while. A lot of discipline on my part was needed. I really had no choice but to rise above my own feelings in order to be as effective as possible.

Some of the saddest times working within the prisons were those times when I would speak with an ex-Kinchela inmate. There were times when guilt would overcome me because I was on the right side of the bars. Had they not been stolen from their parents and subjected to years of cruelty at the Home, perhaps they may not have ended up in a cell with little hope for the future.

Back on The Block

I stood looking at what had once been my home. Not a lot had changed on The Block. The old house was now derelict, and a young woman and her two young children were living under some sheets of tin in the backyard. Once again I was living on Eveleigh Street, and living on Eveleigh Street felt weird. I remember waking up that first morning and having a look around. The Block looked like a bombsite. Derelict buildings. Decay and destruction of property.

People sleeping on the footpaths, in burnt-out buildings. Bricks from crumbling buildings lay around on the footpaths. Broken window glass and beer bottles. Mattresses set up in doorways and under awnings. Graffiti everywhere. Any occupied terrace houses had bars on the windows and doors. Wherever there was space, profanities were scrawled in paint.

The same permanent residents were there, but because Redfern was still a very transient place there were many people there that we didn't know, and even more who needed help of some kind. The drug problem had increased, and bashings, overdoses and general violence had now escalated to being everyday occurrences. It was going to take some adjusting to live here again.

For a while we had lived in a small town on the New South Wales south coast, where I accepted a job as minister, as the church's objectives were directed toward the local Koori population. The job came with a car, a generous wage, a new three-bedroom home, electricity and phone. It meant Katherine would need to give up her job, but it would be an ideal place to raise Sienna and we would be able to enjoy coastal living. It was a very attractive place with seemingly nice people and both Katherine and I had high hopes of a successful ministry.

The car offered was an old bomb that continually broke down. Our electricity bills often went unpaid, and the generous wages were slow at first and then non-existent. As time passed things worsened to the point where Katherine was experiencing bouts of depression and I was at a low point.

These problems stemmed from the fact that I wouldn't prevent a certain man's brother-in-law from attending services. It wasn't my place to tell someone not to attend. The more I refused to ban this man, the worse our situation became. Things became so unpleasant that leaving became the only recourse open to us. The congregation was disappointed to hear that we were leaving but there was no other option.

Redfern had always been in the back of my mind and now I felt it calling me back again. We headed for Sydney, back to The Block.

Sienna was now seven years old, and it was quite a task to keep her from danger. She had to learn a totally different way of living on The Block, and often couldn't comprehend why so many changes to her everyday life became essential. Probably the hardest rule for her to follow was never to go outside without her shoes on because of the used needles and broken glass lying on the ground in the streets and parks. It was a case of treating everything with caution until she was retrained and totally used to her new way of life.

Ray Welsh was the minister employed by the Anglican Church to manage the Crossroads church in Redfern, and it was as his assistant that I started life back at Redfern. He moved around quite a lot so I conducted the weekly services and the breakfast program. I felt very blessed to achieve a first for The Block. On 14 April 2002, two and half years after returning here, I became the first Aboriginal minister on The Block to be commissioned in the Koori Lighthouse Church, the same small church I came to in 1978.

Even though The Block was only 250 metres from the Crossroads, the lifestyle there was very different. The Block was the coalface, the place where it all happened, and it needed a hands-on approach. This was an opportunity for Katherine and me to help many lost souls.

Under the trees up near the top of The Block is the traditional meeting place. It has served this function for over a hundred years. Even though the council had long ago paved the area, fires are lit in the open daily to help everyone keep warm. Broken lounge chairs and milk crates are placed around the fire, and at almost any time of the day people can be found sitting there, some in various stages of intoxication. The fires are alight here night and day and are usually fuelled with wood from furniture and pallets. Under these trees is the hub of The Block. Whenever there's a fight, more often than not it'll be under the trees or very close by. Most of the Kooris who live on The Block pass by that area regularly so it's a common meet-and-greet area.

Our house is on a corner, about forty metres from the trees, which is the main intersection on The Block. It's through here that the people disperse into the different areas within. Most of the residents are without cars and so walk past our house regularly. Quite a few come to our door day or night, looking for help of some kind or just for a chat. Often all they need is a sandwich and they're on their way again. Everyone knows who we are and they know we'll help where we can. From our small porch we can see just about everything so we know when there's trouble brewing. Despite cars being trashed and stolen regularly, our car has never been touched.

The locals are very good to us time-wise. Many of them are up at daybreak, but they always give us until at least seven o'clock before knocking on our door. They're just as considerate at night, usually never coming to our door after ten o'clock, unless it's an emergency. We're sometimes kept awake by a barrage of yelling and swearing, which is more common in the warmer months. Winter tends to wear them down early in the evenings.

One of our biggest worries was life on The Block for Sienna. Despite the needles on the ground, never once has she been pricked or injured in any way. Everyone on The Block knows her, and she plays in the park about twenty metres from the trees, without fear of harm. No-one's ever tried to hurt her even when they're drunk. I believe that God watches over her.

Being where we are gives us the opportunity to assist quickly when necessary, and also allows us to look out for those that are sick or may have overdosed. Overdoses are a common occurrence, and our house is one of the few places with a telephone to call for an ambulance. Ambulances are called to The Block daily, sometimes more than once, depending on the quality of drugs available at any given time.

There are those who are homeless coupled with mental illness, and they need a friendly face to talk to, as they have little connection to others around them.

We hear most of the fights and arguments before we see them. They are mainly fist-fights, but sometimes axes and knives are used. Gunshots are not uncommon throughout the night.

It's no exaggeration to say that The Block has often been an unsafe place for white people who are unaccompanied. Occasionally someone has unknowingly taken a shortcut through there and will be bashed and/or robbed for their trouble. Things have improved since the new community centre opened, but it's still not safe for white women to enter The Block unaccompanied at night, and even driving through there is not advised. Some non-Kooris come there trying to buy drugs but usually end up leaving injured and without their money.

Trust is not something that's extended to many people here and most believe that in everything in life there is an 'us and them' situation. If you're not accepted then you're a 'them'. This applies to all colours and races. It's the same for the police. They're always treated as outsiders, and according to most of the homeless, they are never under any circumstances to be trusted. This is unfortunate as there are some very decent police, but too many locals have had bad experiences with them.

The police have an extremely difficult job to do and it's not made any easier when some of their own behave in a racist manner. As soon as there is a racist remark or incident, the word gets round and results in clashes between the residents and the police. Unfortunately both sides practise racism and some of the people on The Block hate white people to the point where they'll do bodily harm whenever they can. There was a time when I was like that and I can relate to what they feel. Inequality always breeds contempt.

The Block's people are a very hard lot and it's difficult to get close to them. Even though most trust me, a few still keep me at arm's length, just in case I'm not what I seem. Their self-preservation mechanism is very astute. Usually no-one's allowed to penetrate an individual's space. Even those who have slept under the same awning for months still won't trust one another beyond a certain point. More often than not it's a case of 'I have so very little but everyone's still trying to steal it from me.'

Everyone performs as an individual working for his own purposes, until an outside problem faces them. Then they all band together as if they have worked as a close-knit community at all times. When that problem is no longer a threat, it's back to everyone for himself. This makes it so much harder for the police to operate. Any person who robs or assaults somebody from outside is safe on The Block. There is an unbelievable amount of covering for each other, and people will not cooperate with outside autho-rity. If someone is singled out by the police, then everyone rebels, protecting the perpetrator and giving him a solid alibi.

Money is a constant source of problems for the residents. The homeless are recipients of social security of some kind. Even if they wanted a job they lack the skills and basic requirements to obtain one. They have no good clothes, no sense of professional appearance and no address, other than under the tin down the lane.

Keeping their dole payment day a secret is very difficult. Most know when each other's payment is due. On paydays the only way recipients can keep their money for themselves is to be far away from The Block until it's all spent. Only after they're penniless can they return, usually coming back with a small supply of drugs, a full belly and totally inebriated, to face their indignant group of 'friends'. Sharing dole money is not an option, because then they would have to choose who to spend it with. Regardless of who is picked, the unchosen ones will be angry, and so it's just as easy to make themselves scarce and spend it on themselves. Adopting this system creates the problem of being broke two days after they're paid. That leaves them the next twelve days wanting. Meaning they are begging, stealing and going without.

Pressure from relatives is the other problem. Because relations must be respected, if they ask for a 'loan' it must be given if you have the money. The only way to avoid giving your money away is to have none left. The rule is: if you have funds, you lose them, unless you've already spent it all. If you have funds and don't give, then you're ostracised. Lack of respect simply isn't tolerated, and it's difficult to stay in everyone's good books around payday.

Everyone operates independently of each other, but this doesn't apply to the purchase of grog. More often than not, two or three will unite to purchase grog, as there is more buying power. Drinkers pool their money within the group to buy a carton of beer or casks of wine, and then all sit together to drink. Only those who have contributed to the purchase may drink and everyone is expected to drink the same amount. Fights break out if one is getting more than the other. If a friend of the group tries to join in without contributing, he'll be told to go. It seems friendship doesn't extend to receiving free grog. The drinking will continue until the grog is all gone. Groups don't rely on friendship. You may drink with one group one day and another the next, depending on finances.

Unfortunately, food comes a poor last to drugs and grog. Hunger causes many problems, and fights are more likely to start when people have not eaten. Most of the homeless are hungry every day. There are charities that supply meals, but often when they're open is when many people are under the influence and unable to get there. There are some who will not accept charity, believing it robs them of their pride.

Some of the people on The Block have suffered brain damage in varying degrees and are in and out of psychiatric hospitals. Those who attempt suicide are also in the same position. This group of people are admitted for a couple of months and then return to The Block when released and the cycle starts over again. I know of one case where a person has attempted suicide on four occasions. This person is crying out for help, living on the streets, is HIV positive, has low self-esteem and not much hope for the future.

When the Koori mentally ill, suicide cases or homeless enter hospital, visitors are usually nonexistent, except for clergy. Even if these homeless people have friends, the friends are not comfortable going into a hospital to visit. Most people on The Block are aware when someone's in hospital but they will not leave The Block and travel a few suburbs to visit them. The money for fares alone is enough to dismiss the idea, but aside from that, they make it their business not to get too close to anyone else. It's a protection mechanism most seem to have in place which prevents them from getting hurt by others, as well as ensuring others don't rely on them for anything. I did this myself when I was a young fella on The Block and it saved a lot of tears.

Winter is the worst time for the homeless. The nights seem never to end. Some sleep in burnt-out buildings and others will sleep in the railway station until they're moved along. Those under awnings simply get wet. For the homeless life is an hourly struggle for survival and so they do what they deem necessary to stay alive. If someone is hurt during that process then it is their own bad luck. The homeless see themselves as a society of have-nots. They look at the rest of the population and see people who have — they have jobs, they have money, they have possessions, they have houses, they have a friendly environment and most of all they have others who care about them.

The homeless don't see that it's their addictions that ensure they stay the way they are. They don't see that those on the outside have problems of their own; they just see that they themselves are homeless, penniless and Aboriginal. Believing their situation is solely caused because of their colour and not because of other reasons ensures they'll pay out on non-Aboriginals whenever they feel the need.

People on The Block live far below the accepted standard of living, and this situation is not about to change any time soon. Most will die before anything changes in their lives. Those who so badly need our help are in the main ignored and shunned by society.

Many ex-Kinchela boys are living on The Block and have absolutely no hope of changing their prospects, because they haven't the required skills to do so. There is a fella there whose dad had been a Kinchela boy long before my time there. The father felt so tainted by white man that he went straight from Kinchela to The Block so that he would only come into contact with Aboriginals. He has spent the remainder of his life here, raising his son to be bitter. The son raises the grandchildren in the same way.

The forgotten people in Redfern desperately need friendship and interaction with others to show them that someone actually does care. Just talking with these people brings benefits for them. Their lives are so void of affection that the result is anger and hostility to those who happen to get in their way. And it isn't just about old men. Young people in their early teens and those in their thirties are the main problem ages. These are the people who steal to feed their addictions. The wide spectrum of people who need assistance is growing daily and all charities are operating to full capacity.

On Saturday, 14 February 2004 a fifteen-year-old boy named T J Hickey was impaled on a fence post in Redfern and died. Eyewitnesses to the incident say that the boy was being chased by a police van when he crashed his bike into a fence.

There was underlying tension and anger everywhere on The Block. On the Sunday morning I was giving my usual outdoor sermon and I sensed that something was about to erupt. After our meeting was finished and people were milling around eating sandwiches, I noticed a gathering under the tree across from my house, a larger gathering than usual. I felt instinctively that there was a hostile momentum building up. One of our own had died tragically and there were police swarming everywhere. The sight of police is enough to incite anger — let alone a death, which the residents felt was the fault of police. People were angry and full of grief.

That Sunday night the anger turned to violence. Residents came up the street with wheelbarrows full of rocks. I sent my wife and daughter out of The Block to stay elsewhere, as I knew what was about to happen. And in a short space of time it erupted. Bricks, rocks, stones, bottles and lighted missiles were flung at police. When the contents of one wheelbarrow were empty, they'd wheel it away and come back with a fresh supply. The streets were like a battlefield. The Block was like a war zone. Cars were set alight. I wasn't afraid for my own safety that night; I didn't join in the fighting, and if something did happen I know how to protect myself. I've spent enough time in prison and seen enough violence in my own life to know. What I was afraid of were the consequences of all that anger and grief. I do not condone violence, but what people must understand is that this was the way many younger people on The Block vented their grief and sense of outrage. They were showing how much they loved the young boy who had died. The other point to remember is that in our society, the way we look at it is this: you hurt one Aboriginal person, you hurt them all. In my younger and more violent days, I may have joined in myself. These days I have other ways of expressing my anger and grief, but many on The Block have not had the opportunities that I have had in learning how to deal with intense emotions. They reacted in the only way they knew how, and although it is not my way, I identified with their hurt and anger that night.

I was on the phone quite a bit that night. The BBC rang me from London, the Scottish press rang, and various radio stations rang as well. I was criticised by 2UE for saying the The Block looked like something out of Kosovo. They didn't think it was helpful to my own people to describe it in those terms, but I refused to water down the truth. I think I am in a better position than any journalist to describe my own backyard.

Riot in response to the death of T J Hickey.

*

At the coronial inquest into the death of T J Hickey, the ruling issued on 17 August 2004 by New South Wales coroner John Abernethy found that the police were not responsible either directly or indirectly for the young man's death. It came down to definitions of the young boy being 'followed' or 'pursued'. This was a critical distinction, as police regulations prohibit caged vehicles, such as the one that was 'following' the boy, from pursuing suspects, while following someone is considered legitimate. The two police officers that were driving the van elected not to give evidence. Two Aboriginal police liaison officers who claimed to have seen the incident were not called to give evidence. The coroner described as 'regrettable' the fact that the officers driving the van had not been honest from the start of the inquest.

Not only was the finding an outrage to the community, the coroner then went on to criticise the family of the teenager for not speaking to the police. What people must understand here is that no-one on The Block would take such action as they perceive the police in Redfern to be racist and they are aware of the daily harassment of young black males.

In February 2005 a petition with almost three thousand signatures of those wanting the coronial inquest re-opened was presented to New South Wales Attorney General Bob Debus but the then Premier Bob Carr stated that there would be no new inquiry.

*

It is not hard to understand why people are angry and mistrustful. It is not difficult to see why the young on The Block have no respect for the police.

Not long after the funeral of T J, I presided over the memorial for him, as pastor on The Block. It was a difficult day. I had to be very careful what I said. Emotions were still very raw. Anger and hatred were simmering inside many people. I chose my words carefully and spoke about love and compassion. It was not a day for judgement and vengeance, political or social comment. It was a day to remember the young boy and give thanks for his life.

Children should be the hope of society, but many on The Block are stealing and vandalising at the ages of seven and eight. They're headed for a life of crime. Many of them won't receive a proper education and will continue on the way of their parents. Their diets are void of fruit and vegetables, and most children don't sit down to regular meals. There are those who are really trying, but so much is against them that it's difficult to institute change.

Demonstration demanding a re-opening of the inquest into the death of T J Hickey.

It sounds depressing. It *is* depressing. But this is reality. I look at myself like a band-aid, trying to help when and where I can. I can pray for them and conduct their funerals when they die, but society at large has to help in giving people opportunities that will allow them to change and grow.

Into the future

Cows, paddocks, horses, trees, houses, then more houses. It was 2002 and the car headed towards Kempsey. And then a strange thing happened. When we were nearing Kempsey, memories of the past overcame me. The past literally flashed before my eyes. I was ten again, on the road to Kinchela, my brothers in the car, Mr Norris driving in silence. A panic took hold of me. Where are we going, I wanted to ask. Where are we? And then it passed and I looked at the friends I was with in the car. So long ago, and yet the memories are so powerful that they are able to propel themselves into my life decades later and cause my heart to skip a beat. We were on our way to Kinchela for a reunion.

The sounds of the didgeridoo floated over the mid-morning gathering. That morning, the didgeridoo, which for Aboriginal people heralds important occasions, celebrations and tribal rituals, sounded ominous. Apprehension filled the air. Local Dunghutti elder Bluey Smith led the men in a line as they walked solemnly up towards the stage area and took their seats. Welcome home.

It was Saturday, 17 September 2002, and fifty of the boys, now men, stood with over two hundred family and community members on the old Kinchela site. Black and white were there to honour them, to acknowledge their courage and survival, and still others were there to say sorry of behalf of the government for the gross injustice that was inflicted on the Stolen Generations.

People came from everywhere. And there were those present who only had to stroll across the lawn to get there — the Koori residents of the Bennelong Haven Indigenous Drug and Rehabilitation Centre, built on the site where the dormitories once stood. Back where it all started. When I was a Kinchela boy I was shunned in Kempsey, in the hospital and in the community, as were all Koori boys. On this reunion day, we were now treated with respect and admiration. The Mayor of Kempsey, Janet Hayes, welcomed the Dunghutti elders and all the visitors. The Mayor acknowledged on behalf of the Kempsey Shire the hurt, anger and shame that Kinchela boys suffered and still suffer. Reverend John Brown, a Uniting Church minister and co-chair of the Sorry Day Committee and Journey of Healing, congratulated the men on their survival. The Journey of Healing began when elders at Uluru brought home some of their own members of the Stolen Generations and then sent message sticks to all corners of Australia. The message sticks said: 'It is time. Bring them home.'

Today, there is no evidence of what happened here between 1924 and 1970. The old dormitories have long gone, many of the former managers and guards have passed away, government policies have changed, and programs of reconciliation have been implemented. The memories, however, are still there; the hurt has not passed away. Most of the men still carry the results of their childhood experience close to their hearts. Stories similar to mine, stories different to mine, but all tainted by our time at Kinchela. One thing we all had in common was that no-one had escaped lightly. I spoke that day; I told my story. I spoke about the consequences of being stolen and how it ruined many years of my life. I also spoke about being healed by God of the many deeply scarring experiences that had been a part of my life.

*

In 1884 and 1885 the area where Bennelong Haven stands today was known as the Parish of Kinchela, County of Macquarie. The area where the Home was situated was deemed an Aboriginal Reserve. The Kinchela Aboriginal School was started in 1892 at Pelican Island, near the town of Kinchela. It operated for a short time until it closed, only to be reopened in 1911. It later amalgamated with Kinchela Boys' Home opened in 1924 and finally, when the Pelican Island and Fattorini Island schools closed, the school was established on the site where the Home was situated. On 2 July 1923, six girls and two boys were the first enrolments, the number of girls increasing to ten. The girls were later moved to other locations.

Kinchela reunion, 2002.

Some of the first boys to come to Kinchela at that time were boys who had previously lived at the Boys Home and School, George Street, in Singleton. After the closing of the Singleton Boys Home on 15 January 1924, at the order of the Aboriginal Protection Board, most of the boys were sent to Kinchela.

For almost five decades, Kinchela housed and schooled boys and 'trained' them for their future. The Kinchela School Home closed in 1970, and there was much debate about how the property could be put to use. The Aborigines Advisory Council suggested a conference centre, and another Aboriginal group suggested the farm be run on a commercial basis by Aboriginal people. The government advertised the sale of Kinchela on 5 May 1972 but the sale was abandoned. Val Bryant OA held negotiations with the Aboriginal Lands Trust and established what is now known as Bennelong Haven. Val was widely known for her success in running centres in Sydney and for her philosophy of spiritually connecting the whole family of a person who is grog-dependent.

Bennelong Haven is Aboriginal-owned and serves as a rehabilitation facility for people referred by the courts.

*

Going back was an amazing experience. Painful and positive. Depressing and uplifting. It was wonderful to meet up with men whom I hadn't seen for years and it was very sad to hear some of the stories about how their lives had unfolded since Kinchela.

*

Today I spend my time on The Block helping the homeless, the addicted and the very poor. I work with the Baptist, the Anglican and other churches.

My practical function is to assist with the everyday basics of food, shelter and clothes. My emotional interaction comes when offering comfort to those who are not coping with life's difficulties and unfairnesses. My spiritual function is to pray for these people and show them how God can change lives. Katherine and I both act as counsellors, adjudicators, friendly listeners and a multitude of other roles that crop up each day.

We take groups of homeless men on fishing trips and picnics, and on cold nights we collect those asleep in parks and take them to shelters. More than one old man has died from exposure after sleeping on the grass in the park on a very cold night. Once a month we put on a barbecue for all the homeless, fetching men from the Cross and around Woolloomooloo, as well as Redfern. Occasionally we take them around to different places in the city. It's not much, but these get-togethers help to bring a little normality into their otherwise mundane lives.

Our church hasn't the funds to carry out expensive programs, and without the assistance of the Anglicans, the Baptists, the Salvation Army and the Catholics very little would be achieved. Our congregation is very poor and we don't even cover the extra groceries needed each day on The Block. Fortunately Katherine has a good paying job and makes up any shortfall. It's surprising just how much a ham and cheese sandwich can contribute to someone's wellbeing. To send someone back to their home in the bush can cost around $60 and these journeys are an almost daily occurrence. If we don't return them back to their homes, then other costs are incurred, along with the costs of breaking the law when a person is trying to survive in a strange place.

Constantly giving out positive messages to our street congregation tends to sap energy and vitality, and at times the harsh reality of daily life on The Block can still become overwhelming. Katherine and I find we must discipline ourselves to maintain a certain level of aloofness from the lives of others around us. We must be compassionate and yet remind ourselves that the only way we survive is to not let ourselves get too worn down by each individual case.

I wake at four o'clock each morning and spend sixty to ninety minutes reading the Bible and praying. I pray for forgiveness, strength, wisdom and the fortitude I need to carry on each day to help the people on The Block. I believe it's my role to be the go-between, not with each other, but between them and God. They don't ask for his help and guidance, so each morning I ask in their stead. Then as the day goes on, while they go about their business, I believe they're covered.

I wouldn't be speaking truthfully if I said I never felt unappreciated and sometimes even ineffective. I, like so many others, need to feel as though our efforts are not in vain. Nothing is worse than feelings of rejection, and during my lifetime I've often felt as if I have been passed over. Not long after I returned to The Block, I often wondered if this was where I was meant to be. It's sometimes necessary to receive confirmation for me to just hang in there.

But good things have happened since I have come back to work on The Block, not in any material sense, but rather by the fact that I have been rewarded with opportunities. I have had the chance to travel overseas as a representative of my people. In Samoa in March 2004 I went as a representative of Aboriginal people to the Inter-Religious and International Peace Council, and in August of the same year I travelled to Jerusalem for the Heart to Heart For Peace Conference, where three thousand people from all over the world came together. I went as the Peace Ambassador for Aboriginal People and as a representative of the Stolen Generations.

I spent ten days in Fiji visiting two prisons and preaching in three churches, and I also visited Hawaii for an event called The Gathering where Indigenous peoples from all over the world met for prayers, worship and fellowship. Hawaii was the furthermost I'd been from home, and I made sure my time there was well spent. Hawaii was a powerful experience. I sent a message to the other Indigenous peoples at the gathering, a message of hope for the future when we'll no longer be looked down on, and the time will come when the Indigenous churches will be raised up to the same levels as the many big-name churches in non-Indigenous communities. A time when we'll look at non-Indigenous people knowing that we're their equal, with equal opportunities and equal rights. I gave this word to the Indigenous peoples from seventeen countries, and it was wonderful to look out and see them standing together with pride.

When the Fijian Prime Minister came to Australia for a visit, I was asked to represent the Indigenous people and welcome him to Australia. Although it was an honour sitting next to the Prime Minister, I reminded myself that there are people on The Block who, with the right resources and assistance, could be wonderful ambassadors for their country.

I have never had the funds to be able to travel overseas and it is only with the assistance of the churches and people's donations that I have been able to go to different places to represent my people.

There are many Kinchela men living in Redfern and many members of the Stolen Generation who have not yet recovered from what happened in the past, and today are still unable to comprehend why it happened. This lack of understanding and the grief many still experience is preventing them from moving ahead with their lives. Many are as yet unable to leave this very distressing and extraordinarily cruel part of their lives behind them. It affects the way they go about their everyday life, how they raise their children and the way they treat their wives and partners. Wives and partners of Kinchela men suffer much, and usually women cannot stay with a Kinchela man.

I am one of a group who assist on The Block. Over the years Redfern has been well served by some very good men such as Jack Braeside, Bill Byrd and Dick Blair, who helped those in need of assistance on The Block. It was a comfort knowing these men were here, more than willing and usually very able to help. During my life I've never sought large amounts of money for the work I do, however it is nice to occasionally have our efforts acknowledged. It's taken a long time, but now that our work here is becoming known people have supported us. Every charitable dollar is scarce these days. It's surprising what quarter donations will come from sometimes. These unexpected, helping hands provide the invaluable assistance we always need.

I am kept busy with my ministry in the jails, assisting prisoners and their families. One night a week I hold a meeting in my home for those battling drug and grog addictions, and on another night I hold a counselling night. On Sundays I do three church services. One is held outside my house on a spare allotment. Chairs are provided outside but many prefer to listen from the safety of their own space. They can hear us all over The Block because of the loudspeakers. Over the years we've had many tent gatherings there as well. At times, when I don't think anyone has taken notice of anything, someone will surprise me by coming to talk about something that they have heard me say.

A few weeks ago I was officially ordained in the Aboriginal Pentecostal Church.

I'm at a certain stage now regarding Kinchela, and because of that, I am now in the position to help those who haven't yet reached that stage. Some never will reach it. I don't mean I'm over it; I just deal with it in ways that are not self-destructive. I am also at the point where I can forgive. That doesn't mean that I don't have a sense of outrage and injustice regarding what happened to my people. I've experienced the horror that was Kinchela, like so many who came before and after me, and I believe I can assist my brothers and sisters of the Stolen Generation to put this degrading and humiliating part of our lives behind us.

Being taken from my parents at such an early age has had its consequences. I often wonder where I'd be had I remained under my father's guidance. It's impossible not to go through the list of 'ifs'. If only I had been allowed to stay with my family. If only Dad had been home that day. If only I had been told the reason why my mother didn't fight for us that day. Before Kinchela, I had an average lifestyle and the possibility of growing up in a loving family environment. After Kinchela I was well into my thirties before I got back on track again. This period in the lives of stolen boys dominates to a different degree in each of us, depending on the afflictions while incarcerated, our character development, our opportunities and behaviour since our release. I still carry painful memories from that period of incarceration, and try as I may I can't get it all out of my system. Perhaps one day I will be completely free of that part of my life.

I believed very strongly that Prime Minister John Howard needed to say sorry to the Stolen Generations. Yes, it does seem to be the hardest word. The simple act of saying sorry is, for some, healing. It takes courage to say sorry. It would have taken more courage to say sorry and to have lost votes as well. Kevin Rudd has done it now, but saying sorry isn't enough. The Stolen Generations need to be compensated. Aboriginal boys and girls who were stolen worked for years for nothing on farms, dairies and cattle stations all over this country. Their money was put into 'trust funds'. They never saw one cent of it. Some asked about all their unclaimed money and were told that the records of what they earned were destroyed in a fire in the Sydney Archives. These people still live in poverty today. There is a verse in Proverbs that says, 'Where there is no vision, the people perish.' Many Aboriginal people have no hope or vision of the future.

Just because I became a Christian doesn't mean that I don't feel anger or have personal problems. There are issues that I still struggle with today that are a direct result of Kinchela. I have a problem with being told what to do. I buck against authority.

To this day I still have a problem with the relationship I had with my mother. I understand that she was powerless that day we were taken. I understand the history and the policies of the day, the government ideologies. I know it all. But even so, there is a part of me that can't accept what she did that day.

Sorry Day, 2008.
Bill Simon meets
Kevin Rudd.

I have never quite got a hold of the normal mother-and-son bond. It was early one morning over forty-six years ago when I called out to her to help, but she never came. Logically I know that she was simply unable to protect us from the welfare men, but it was too late, the memory of her standing there letting us be taken from our home was firmly planted in my mind from that time on. The guards at Kinchela clinched it; constantly telling us the only reason we were there was because our mothers and fathers didn't want us. That sentence was burned into my brain, and to my everlasting despair I have not been able to remove it: not with logic, not with informed reason and not even with the power of prayer. It shames me to think that with all these weapons at my disposal, things between my mother and I could not be fully repaired. I tried as hard as I could and so did she, but it never worked.

My mother had a close relationship with Katherine and told her that it was like a knife being ripped through her when they took her children away. Katherine tried to tell me this, but my stubbornness prevented me from being convinced. It hurt my mother when the welfare made out we were neglected. The story they told in court was that my father was neglecting us because he wasn't at home. They never bothered to mention he was working in the forest near Raymond Terrace about thirty kilometres from home that day. Instead of thinking that this was a good man for doing whatever needed to be done to support his family, they condemned him for not being at home all the time.

My mother became seriously ill in 1995 and spent some time in hospital. During the last two weeks of her stay my family took her out to Karuah where she was given traditional healing medicine. She then went into remission, went back to her home, and lived for another eight months, astounding the doctors. She died on 29 February 1996 in the Mater Hospital and was buried at Newcastle. I conducted her funeral. It took years but I grew to love my mother, and there is a deep sadness concerning the early years when we missed out on being together. There will always be residual guilt about hating her for such a long time, but my love for her outweighs any negative emotions these days.

There are others, no longer here, whose loss I feel deeply. I was devastated by the death of my cousin Boxy, who had always been there for me. He was my playmate as a child, my protector in prison, my friend. Boxy had the contract on my life lifted. Life was unkind to Boxy as he grew older. He spent most of his time in jail, approximately twenty-five years in total, and he was always a model prisoner, held in good stead by the other prisoners and by the guards as well.

During one of his visits to my mother's house Boxy turned up to see me. He was in extreme turmoil and he spoke of spirits following him everywhere. We talked and prayed together as I tried to understand what he was going through. At the time he seemed to have many problems running around in his head. After talking throughout the night he seemed a little better. The next day I went back to Redfern and thought no more about it. Then

Bill Simon and his mother Grace Simon before her death in 1996.

I received the news that Boxy had locked himself in a room and had hung himself. Sadly I hadn't spent enough time with him on my last visit to know exactly what was going on in his mind. To this day I wonder if there was more I could've done for him. I suppose I'll never know now, but what I do know is that I'll never stop missing him.

In the same year Boxy died, my youngest brother Lenny came to live with me. As he suffered from epilepsy it wasn't a good idea for him to live by himself. His epilepsy was under control most of the time but his drinking problem was out of control. One day he told me he was sick of being a drunk and fed up with the life he was leading. He asked me to help him so I took him over to a nearby Alcoholics Anonymous meeting. They suggested that Lenny be put into Bennelong Haven, a place for alcoholics to dry out.

I didn't know it at the time of Lenny's admission, but Bennelong Haven had a very sinister past. It hadn't always been a place of healing. Bennelong Haven was just a new name for what used to be the Kinchela Boys' Home. Many members of the Stolen Generations were alcoholics in later life because of their experiences there, and then, to cure them of their addiction,

Brothers Bill and Murray Simon in 1975.

they were sent back to the very place where their troubles began. A different name did nothing to change the haunting memories that place held for so many. A court order took Lenny from his mother and institutionalised him. A court order sent him back to an institution, however well-intentioned, and he died there.

I never saw Lenny again after he went to Bennelong Haven. He died from injuries he received after being hit on the head with a brick in an altercation. I went up to Bennelong Haven and brought his body back to Newcastle. I conducted the funeral of own my brother. My mother took Lenny's death very hard. After the funeral there was talk of a payback on the man that had killed my brother. This man was imprisoned for my brother's death, but payback could have been arranged. As the family elder, I said there was to be no payback. It will stop here, I told them. It was difficult

Bill Simon and his daughter Vicky on The Block.

to find forgiveness for this man, but I asked them to believe that it was not for us to administer punishment. There had been too many deaths already. Leave it up to the big fella upstairs, I said.

My early experiences shaped my life. The consequences have hurt many who have been a part of my journey. I have written to the women in my life that I have hurt and asked for their forgiveness. They have accepted my apology and have forgiven me and for that I am truly grateful. I am in contact with my son that I had with Phoebe and his two children, my grandchildren.

My brothers' and cousins' lives have been negatively impacted upon because their experience of being taken and incarcerated. I have a brother who is in jail for a serious crime and other cousins who are also doing time for different crimes. My brothers Murray and David weren't able to contribute to this story as they felt it

Bill Simon in front of posters: Kinchela Boys Home: 'Why', and Sorry Day, 2008.

was better left alone. I have an obligation to respect their privacy and so haven't detailed too much about my extended family. My family and I are not unique. They have many of the problems facing Indigenous people all over the country. There are those in my family who, like myself, have dedicated their lives to helping our own. My aunt Ella Simon, who was born on Purfleet, is well known for her book *Through My Eyes*, which details her life assisting Koori people.

My sense of humour gets me through the days. My co-authors, in one of their many interviews with me, asked if I had any skills when I left Kinchela in the areas of cooking, shopping, banking, budgeting, paying bills, connecting electricity, that sort of thing.

'Did you know how to do those things?' they asked.

'I still don't!' I said.

I've made judges laugh, police and prison wardens laugh, violent and depressed criminals laugh, Kooris and non-Kooris alike. I made Ivan Milat laugh, and that's not an easy thing to do. I made inmates laugh when I was locked up with them, and I make them laugh now when I visit them. I marry them, bury them, baptise their children and laugh with them. Simply, I try to bring a little hope into their lives. Interesting things happen to me when I least expect them to. Last year I landed a part in a crowd scene in Baz Luhrmann's film *Australia*.

I have little connection to the traditional ways. They were lost to my parents and they were lost to me. My Aboriginal language was discouraged. I don't know much about the Dreamtime stories or feel any great attachment to the traditional ways as I haven't really explored them. My reality is that of an urban Koori man out there helping other Kooris in a harsh urban landscape. Aboriginals have the knowledge and ability to know how to survive in unfriendly times and in hard conditions. We survived Kinchela and we will continue to survive.

Had it not been for God's help, I would've been dead long ago from grog, violence or drugs, but here I am at fifty-nine years of age giving back to my people. I will continue to assist my brothers and sisters of the Stolen Generations to put this degrading and humiliating part of our lives behind us and build a better life.

My life's journey has been a bumpy road and it's not over yet. It's with these thoughts that I move forward, helping those who have drifted off the pathway and hopefully restoring some dignity to those men who suffered with me all those years ago. There are times when I wake up and wonder what on earth I am doing — but I know, deep down, The Block, the heart of Redfern, is where I'm meant to be.

Index

Aboriginal culture, *see* culture
Aboriginal Foundation, at Central, 76
Aboriginal Lands Trust, 149
Aboriginal language, 3, 161
Aboriginal Pentecostal Church of Jesus Christ, Redfern, 112, 153
Aboriginal Protection Board, 2, 31, 149
Aborigines Advisory Council, 149
Aborigines Welfare Board, 11, 31, 44, 53, 54, 68
    correspondence about Bill, 73; school report, 47
    removal of Simon brothers, 13–20, 21
    rules outlawing traditional life, 3–5
    staff visits to Kinchela, 34, 51, 56
abuse at Kinchela, 41
    see also punishment at Kinchela
acid, 97–9
addiction, *see* alcohol; drugs; gambling; smoking
aggression, 57, 61, 65
    arrests for, 58, 67, 68
    Bill's father's attitude towards, 12
    boys in Kinchela, 37, 45, 46
    see also bashings; fights
alcohol (grog), 141–2
    Bennelong Haven, 148–50; Lenny in, 157–8
    Bill's father's attitude towards, 6
    Bill's work and ministry, 112, 123–4, 139, 153
    Catholic priest at Kinchela, 60
    Richard, 120
    Uncle Jim, 49, 70, 87
alcohol (grog), Bill's addiction to, 64–5, 70, 71, 74–86, 89, 92
    drink-driving charges, 85–6, 110–11
    ending, 97–101, 102, 104, 105, 110–11
    living with Lilly, 79–83, 102
    methylated spirits, 77, 78
    money spent on, 75–6, 77, 83, 84
Anglicans, 60, 112–13, 129, 138
apologies, 58, 159
    to Stolen Generations, 154
armed robbery, 68, 93–4
arrests, 58, 67, 113, 114
    Bill's cousins, 100, 101, 118
    drink-driving, 85–6, 111
    evasion, 100
assault charge, 58
assimilation policy, 3, 29, 31, 45
aunts, 6, 81
    Deb, 9, 18
    Maree (Hexham), 78–9, 86, 87
    Maree (Redfern), 74, 76
    May, 75
    Simon, Ella, 160
Australia, 161

Bankstown, 63–9, 73–4
Bankstown Jail, 67
baptism, 101
Baptists, 150
bashings, 137, 139
    by Bill, 65, 76, 92; Lilly, 80
    of Bill, 93
bed wetting, 22, 24, 27, 28–9, 45
Bennelong Haven Indigenous Drug and Rehabilitation Centre, 147, 148–59
    Lenny in, 157–8
BHP, 79
bibles, 64, 98, 151
    Uncle Jim's, 48
bikies, 65, 67

Index

Biripi people, 3, 6, 71
births, 3
   Bill's brothers, 5, 11
   Bill's children, 81, 82, 88, 89, 129
   see also fatherhood
Black Duck Tribe, 3
Black Theatre, 102, 109, 112
Blacktown, 102–3, 104–6
Blair, Dick, 108, 111
   working with, 102, 109–10, 115, 128
The Block, *see* Redfern and The Block
boils, 52–3
bomb making, 86
boots, 24, 27
Borland, Mr (Kinchela manager), 20, 22, 24, 52, 58
   Christmas time, 56
   comments about Uncle Jim, 49
   hypocrisy, 53
   instruction on friendships with other Koori boys, 47
   missing boys, 40–1, 54
   punishment parade, 27, 31–2, 33, 35–6, 56–7; Bill's, 41–3, 55
Borland, Mrs, 53
Botany, 109
boxing, 35, 45
   Bill's father, 9–10, 11–13, 72
   Uncle Jim, 48–9
Boxy, 10, 13, 86, 94–5
   death, 156–7
   in jail with, 67–8, 95
Braeside, Reverend Jack, 112
brainwashing at Kinchela, 37–8, 44–6, 49–51
breakouts from Kinchela, 40–1
   Bill's, 53–5
Brisbane, 12, 80, 82–5, 88–9, 106–8
Broadmeadow, 86, 92
   church, 127
   detention centre, 133
brothers, 5, 72–3, 79, 97
   Tony, 99, 104, 110, 113; swapping car seats with, 85–6, 111
   see also Simon, David; Simon, Lenny; Simon, Murray
brothers at Kinchela, 40, 45, 46
   Darby boys, 38–9
   Matthew and Robert, 61, 65–6
   twins Perry and Joel, 56
   'Walkin' down the line', 35–6
Brown, Coogan, *see* Simon, Uncle Jim
Brown, Reverend John, 148
Bryant, Val, 149

'Bully Boys', 46
Burnum Burnum, 46
Byrd, Mr, 37

canings, 27, 28, 31–4, 46, 57
   Bill's, 42–4, 55
car accidents, 78–9
   Bill's, 106–8, 114
cars, 74, 109, 120, 137, 139
   drink-driving charges, 85–6, 110–11
   Matthew's, 65–7
Carter, Isaiah (Ike), 3–13, 23, 48, 50, 72, 73
   brother Shane, 11, 100, 101, 104
   court case following Bill's removal, 17–18, 70, 156
   death, 59, 67–8, 72, 76
   friends of, 77, 85, 87
   separation from Grace, 70–1, 72
   sister Maree, 74, 76
   work, 9, 11, 156; boxing for shows, 9–10, 11–13, 72
Carter, Shane, 11, 100, 101, 104
Catholic priest at Kinchela, 60
Cessnock, 129
Cessnock Prison, 132
chicken stealing, 12
Child Welfare Act, 54
Child Welfare Department, 59, 63, 64
Christianity, 98–9, 100–5, 108–15, 121, 123–4
   baptism, 101
   bibles, 64, 98, 151; Uncle Jim's, 48
   Blair's church and church work in Redfern, 102, 109–10, 112, 115, 128
   Crossroads Anglican church, 112–13, 138
   at Kinchela, 60
   ministry, 127, 128–47, 150–4
   Mount Druitt church, 101–2, 103, 104–5, 108–9
   Newcastle area, 113, 114, 127, 129–36
   ordination, 153
   prison ministry, 111, 114, 129–36, 152, 153, 160
   at Purfleet, 2, 5
   Simon family, 6, 48, 110
Christmas
   at Kinchela, 56
   at Saltwater, 6–7
churches, *see* Christianity
cigarettes, 60, 99, 102, 108, 111, 118
'Classy Coogan', 48

Index

cleanliness at Kinchela, 22, 24, 30, 32
  washing bedclothes and sheets, 27, 28–9
clothes, 64, 65, 113
  first time in church, 100
clothes at Kinchela, 22, 29, 56
  footwear, 24, 27, 46
  Kempsey High students, 30, 46
coal dust, 43
colonisation, 2
colour of skin, 37, 38–9
community work, 111–13, 117, 118–25, 138–9
  with Dick Blair's organisation, 102, 109–10, 112, 128
  at Kinchela, 58, 59–60
compensation of Stolen Generations, 154
confinement at Kinchela, 33–4, 36–7
contract to kill Bill, 94–5
Coolah pub, 77
Cooper, Albert, 26
Cootamundra Girls' Home, 40
court cases, 58, 67, 68
  drink-driving charges, 86, 111
  to separate Bill and brothers from parents, 17–18, 61, 70–1
cousins, 6, 70
  Ella, 78
  Gilbert, 97–8, 99–100, 101, 104–5, 110
  Harry, 99–100, 104–5, 110
  visit to The Block, 117–18
  see also Boxy
cowboys and Indians, 12, 50–1
criminal activities, 67, 68, 86, 92–5
  see also jail; robbery
Crossroads Anglican church, 112–13, 138
cruelty, see punishment at Kinchela
Crump, Kevin, 134–5
culture, 3–5, 6, 9, 71, 89, 161
  methods used to alienate Kinchela boys from, 29, 37, 44–51

dairy work at Kinchela, 24, 27, 57
Darby brothers, 38–9
daughters, 86, 88–90, 92, 131
  Sienna, 129, 130, 137–8, 139
  see also Simon, Vicky
deaths, 78–9, 123, 124
  Bill's brothers, 5, 158–9
  Bill's father, 59, 67–8, 72, 76
  Bill's mother, 156

Boxy, 156–7
Hickey, T J, 143–6
  people wanting to kill Bill, 94–5;
Tim, 57, 122
Uncle Jim, 87, 98
demonstrations and protests, 120–1, 143–6
disabled boys at Kinchela, 39–40
dormitories at Kinchela, 22–4, 25, 27–9
  pranks in, 41–4
  roll calls, 40
'down the line', 35–7
drinking, see alcohol
drugs and drug addiction, 100, 122, 137, 139, 141, 142
  Bill's, 92–4, 97–9, 101
  Bill's work and ministry, 102, 111, 112, 117, 153
  non-Kooris coming to buy, 140
Duck, Mr, 10

ears, hitting around, 37
education, 2
  Bill's, 29–30, 47, 57; Kendall school, 9
  at Kinchela, 25, 29–30, 56–7, 149–50
  see also Kempsey High students
employment, 2, 3, 29
  Bill's father, 9, 10, 11, 156; boxing in shows, 9–10, 11–13, 1072
  Uncle Jim, 48–9
  see also work boys
employment, Bill's, 75, 76, 77, 84, 89–90
  BHP steel, 79
  box trailer maker, Bankstown, 61, 64, 68, 73, 74
  as handyman, 113, 127
  house painting, 111
  at Kinchela, 24, 27, 30–1, 57; in local community, 58
  labouring, 58, 85, 109, 113
  market gardening, 73
  minister, 127, 128–47, 150–4
  spindling yarn factory, 78, 79
  spray-painting, 91, 92, 102
  spraying kangaroo hides, 109
  see also community work
epilepsy, 13, 157
escape from Kinchela, 40–1
  Bill's, 53–5
Eveleigh Street, Redfern, 75, 112, 114–15, 118–21, 136–9

164

faith, *see* Christianity
families of Kinchela boys, 29, 45, 49–51, 60
   guards' talking with boys about, 29, 38, 49–50
   release back to, after coming of age, 53
   see also brothers at Kinchela; Simon family
farm work at Kinchela, 24, 27, 30, 57
father, *see* Carter, Isaiah
fatherhood, 80–92, 102–9, 131
   Caitlin and Shauna, 88–92
   Maddie's abortion, 121
   Phoebe's child, 105–6, 108–9, 159
   Richard and Vicky, 80–9, 102–4, 107–8
   Sienna, 129, 130, 137–8, 139
feet, 24, 27, 100
fights, 65, 67, 77
   on The Block, 138, 139, 142; argument between Bill's cousins and landlady, 118
   at Kinchela, 44–6
   with Lilly, 80, 82, 83
   with Phoebe, 105
   at Platts Estate home, 12
   over Susie, 86
   with Susie, 90, 91–2
   see also bashings; boxing
Fiji, 152
films, 10, 161
fire, 88
fish head outfit prank, 41–3
fishing, 1, 3–5, 10, 78, 87, 150
Five Dock, 102, 104
food, 2, 6, 75, 76, 77–8
   goanna, 71
   at Kendall, 10
   at Platts Estate, 11–12
   at Purfleet, 1, 3–5
   see also community work; meals at Kinchela
footwear, 24, 27
   school shoes, 46
forestry work, 9, 10, 11, 156
Foursquare church, Toronto, 127

gambling, 75, 76, 83, 84, 89–90, 94, 99
   ending of addiction, 99, 101
   Richard, 120
games, 12
Gateshead, 127
Gladesville, 91

goanna, 71
government policy, 3, 29, 31, 45
grandparents, 6
   grandfather, 70, 71, 72
   Granny Doris (Nan), 9, 10, 98
   great-great-grandfather, 3
grog, *see* alcohol
guards in jail, 68, 131, 133, 135, 156
guards in Kinchela, 22, 23–4, 27, 30–1, 52, 56
   Bill and Matthew's visit after their release, 66–7
   Bill's complaint to after Lenny hit, 58–9
   checking for wet beds, 28–9
   comments about black people, 37, 49–50
   comments about boys' families, 29, 38, 49–50, 51
   encouraging fights among boys, 44–6
   punishment parade, 32, 33, 37–8, 42–4; Darby boys, 39
   roll calls, 29, 40
   see also Pooley, Mr
Gulargambone, 77
gumboots, 24, 27
guns, 69, 123
   armed robbery, 68, 93–4
   shotgun visit to Redfern, 95–6

haircuts at Kinchela, 22, 46
'Hairy Man', 5–6
Hawaii, 152
Hayes, Janet, 148
health
   after car accident, 106–8
   after jumping from second-floor window, 100
   boils, 52–3
   Kinchela medical examination, 22
   see also hospital patients
hearing, 37
Heart to Heart for Peace Conference, 151–2
hepatitis C, prison inmate with, 133–4
Hermann, Mr, 5, 60
Hexham, 78–9
   Bill's father's death, 67–8, 72
Hickey, T J, 143–6
high school, *see* Kempsey High students
homeless people, *see* community work
hospital patients, 142
   Bill, 52–3, 100, 106–7

Index

Bill's ministry among, 133–5, 136
Lenny, 157–9
hotels, *see* alcohol
house fire, 88
Howard, John, 154
humour, sense of, 160
hunting, 2, 3–5, 77

infidelity of Susie, 91–2, 95–6
Inter-Religious and International Peace Council, 151

jail, 87, 100, 123, 128
  Bill in, 58, 67–8, 95, 111, 114
  Bill's ministry in, 111, 114, 129–36, 152, 153, 160
jealousy, 73, 80
Jerusalem, 151–2
jobs, *see* employment
Journey of Healing, 148

kadaija man in prison, 134
Karuah, 78, 156
Kattang language, 3
Kempsey, 55
  see also Kinchela Boys Home
Kempsey High students, 30, 35, 46–7
  Bill, 47, 57, 61
  punishment, 34
Kempsey Hospital, 52–3
Kempsey Show, 48–9
Kendall, 9–11
Kinchela Boys Home, 20–62, 148–1150
  not telling Lilly about, 83–4
  return with Matthew to *see* brothers, 66–8
  telling Katherine about, 127–8, 129
  thoughts about when intoxicated, 64–5
Kinchela Boys Home ex-boys, 26, 32–3
  ear trouble, 37
  in jail, 136
  psychiatric patient, 135
  Redfern residents, 74, 124, 143, 152
  reunion 2002, 147–50
  Tim, 57, 122
Kings Cross, 64, 65, 75, 125, 150
kitchen duties at Kinchela, 30, 34, 57
Knowles, Minister, 108
Kooma Christian Church, 128
Koori Lighthouse Church, 138

La Perouse, 74–5
labouring, 59, 85, 109, 113
language, 3, 29, 161

speaking in tongues, 101
letters sent to Kinchela, 50
  from Bill's mother, 59, 71
lifesavers, 60
Long Bay Jail, 131, 132
  Bill in, 67–8, 111
LSD, 97–9

Maitland, 78, 130
Maitland Jail, 100, 130–2
marijuana, 92–4
market gardening, 73
Marr, Uncle Berty, 5
marriage, *see* relationships with women
Mayfield, 128–9
meals at Kinchela, 29, 45–6, 56
  eating everything on plate, 56
  kitchen duties, 30, 34, 57
  missing, 32, 45
  in solitary confinement, 33, 34
meals for destitute people, *see* community work
medical examination at Kinchela, 22
Melbourne, 121
memory loss, 106–8
mental health patients, 134–5, 136, 142
methylated spirits, 77, 78, 87
Milat, Ivan, 134, 160
milking at Kinchela, 24, 27, 57
mission life, 1–9, 11
money, 74–6, 86
  for The Block ministry, 118–20, 122, 150–1
  The Block residents, 141–2
  box trailer maker wage, Bankstown, 64, 65–6, 68
  compensation for Stolen Generations, 154
  from drug sales, 92–3
  pocket money in Kendall, 10
  running out in Melbourne, 121–2
  as south coast minister, 137
  spent on gambling, 75, 83, 89–90, 94
  spent on grog, 75–6, 77, 83, 84
  see also employment; robbery
Moore, Rob, 129
Morisset, 134
morning parade at Kinchela, 27, 28, 29
mother, *see* Simon, Grace
Mount Druitt church, 101–2, 103, 104–5, 108–9
Mount Gravatt, 106
Mudgee, 77
Musgrave Park, 83
Muswellbrook, 132

Newcastle area, 77–80, 84–91, 92–100, 113–14, 126–36
    Bill's father's death, 67–8, 72
    Bill's mother's death, 156
    at Bill's mother's place, 79–80, 81–2, 85–6, 88–91, 92–3, 97–100
    Platts Estate, 11–15, 18, 51, 71, 87
    visits to *see* family, 110, 113, 118, 125; to introduce Phoebe, 105
Newcastle City Council, 113
Newcastle Gas Company, 85
Newcastle Hospital, 72
Newtown, 100
Norris, Mr, 15–20
Norris, Mrs, 15, 16
number given at Kinchela, 20, 22, 29, 40

'One Day at a Time', 108
ordination, 153
overseas travel, 151–2

paedophilia, 123–4
parades at Kinchela, 27, 28, 29, 31–44
parents, *see* Carter, Isaiah; Simon, Grace
Parramatta Road car accidence, 114
Penrith, Harry, 46
petrol bomb making, 86
photograph of Uncle Jim, 49
Pilliga Scrub Mission boys, 38–9
Platts Estate, 11–15, 18, 51, 71, 87
police, 40, 55, 95, 107, 121
    Reed, Sergeant, 58, 59
    when Simon brothers taken away, 14, 17, 18–19
    visits after fights with Lilly, 80, 82
    see also arrests
police on The Block, 75, 118, 121, 140
    Bill's relations with, 118, 122
    death of T J Hickey, 143–6
polio, 39–40, 105
Pooley, Mr, 22, 42, 43
    boxing, 35, 45
    'Bully Boys', 46
    punishment administered by, 33, 37
    radio, 53
pranks and practical jokes, 41–4, 57, 122
    by Bill's father, 72
prayer meetings, 101, 102, 104
prefect system at Kinchela, 46, 47, 48, 55
presents, 64
    at Kinchela, 56

Princess Alexandra Hospital, 106–7
prison, *see* jail
prostitutes, 117, 125
protests and demonstrations, 120–1, 143–6
psychiatric patients, 124–5, 126, 142
pubs, *see* alcohol
punishment at Kinchela, 24, 28, 31–44, 55–7
    shoes on after school hours, 46
    wet beds, 27, 28–9
punishment room at Kinchela, 33–4, 36–7
Purfleet Mission, 1–9, 11, 50–1, 160

Queensland, 12, 80, 82–5, 88–9, 106–8

Radio Redfern, 109
rations, 3–5
Redfern and The Block, 90, 109–26, 136–47, 150–3
    death of T J Hickey, 143–6
    medical centre work, 111–12
    ministry, 150–3
    relatives living in, 68, 74; at Auntie Maree's house, 74, 75–6
    visits to from Newcastle, 95–6, 128
    visits to Newcastle from, 113–14, 125
    working with Crossroads Anglican church, 112–13, 138
    working with Dick Blair's organisation, 102, 109–10, 112, 115, 128
Redfern Park protest rally, 120
Reed, Sergeant, 58, 59
relationships with women, 81, 92, 94, 125
    Katherine, 127–30, 137–8, 150–1, 156
    Lilly, 79–85, 88–9, 102–3, 107–8
    Maddie, 121
    Phoebe, 105–6, 108–9, 159
    Susie, 86–92, 95–6
relatives, *see* Simon family
release from Kinchela, 53, 61–2
religion, *see* Christianity
removal from family, 14–20, 61, 70–1
reprogramming at Kinchela, 37–8, 44–6, 49–51
reunion with family, 68–73
    Murray's, 76–7
riots, 121, 143–6
robbery, 75, 76, 92
    armed, 68, 93–4
    stealing cases of spirit, 99–100
    stealing chickens, 12

167

Index

robbery on The Block, 122, 139–40
  by Bill, 75, 76
  returning bags to The Block police, 118
roll calls at Kinchela, 29, 40
Rosebuds, Newcastle, 85–6
roster system at Kinchela, 31
Rudd, Kevin, 154, 155
rules at Kinchela, 22, 30–3, 37–8, 58
  eating everything on plate, 56
  footwear, 24, 30
  friendships with non-Kinchela Koori boys, 47
  roll calls, 29, 40
  see also punishment at Kinchela
runaways, 18–19
  from Kinchela, 40–1; Bill, 53–5
Rutherford, 130

Saltwater, 6–7
Samoa, 151
Sands, Dave, 10
school, *see* education
Seaton, Mr, 27
secondary school, *see* Kempsey High students
sense of humour, 160
sexual abuse at Kinchela, 41
sexual relationships, *see* relationships with women
shoes, 24, 46
shotguns, 95–6
Simon, David, 5, 113, 128, 159–60
  move to Redfern, 110
  removal to and at Kinchela, 14–24, 27–9, 51, 52, 54–5, 60, 61; after Bill's release, 66, 67, 76
Simon, Ella, 1160
Simon, Grace, 48, 51, 78, 154–6, 157, 159
  Bill's childhood, 3, 5–6, 9, 10–11, 13, 51
  Bill's periods of living with, 79–80, 81–2, 85–6, 88–91, 92–3, 97–100
  Bill's removal, 14–15, 16; court case following, 17–18, 61, 70–1
  Bill's reunion with, 68–73
  cooking, 1, 10
  family, *see* Simon family
  letters to Bill in Kinchela, 59, 71
  Murray's reunion with, 76–7
Simon, Uncle Jim, 48–9, 86–7
  death, 87, 98
  at Gulargambone, 77
  at Hexham, 78, 87
  at Wellington, 69, 70, 71, 72, 76
Simon, Lenny, 11, 110, 157–9
  at Kinchela, 51–2, 54–5, 58, 60, 61; after Bill's release, 66, 67, 76
  removal from family, 14–19, 21, 23
Simon, Lilly, 79–85, 88–9, 102–3, 107–8
Simon, Luke, 5
Simon, Murray, 5, 85, 113, 158, 159–60
  meeting with Bill after release from Kinchela, 76–7
  removal to and at Kinchela, 14–24, 27–8, 51, 52, 54–5, 60, 61; after Bill's release, 66
  visits to Redfern, 76, 110, 124–5
Simon, Richard, 81, 82, 84–5, 88–9
  Bill's visit in Brisbane, 107–8
  Lilly's return to Bill in Sydney, 102, 103–4
  living with Bill on The Block, 120, 121–2, 123
Simon, Vicky, 82, 84–5, 87–9, 120, 159
  Bill's visit in Brisbane, 107–8
  Lilly's return to Bill in Sydney, 102, 103–4
Simon family, 3
  in Gulargambone, 77
  in Newcastle area, 77–9, 81–2, 85–7, 125; Kendall, 9, 18
  in Redfern, 68, 74
  Saltwater Christmases, 6–7
  in Wellington, 69–73, 76–7
  see also aunts; brothers; Carter, Isaiah; cousins; Simon, Grace; uncles
Singleton Boys Home, 149
sisters, 72–3, 79, 97
skin colour, 37, 38–9
Smith, Bluey, 147
smoking, 60, 99, 102, 108, 111, 118
solitary confinement at Kinchela, 33–4, 36–7
sons, 1159
  see also Simon, Richard
south coast, 137
South-West Rocks, 53, 57, 59–60
South-West Rocks Jail, 58
speaking in tongues, 101
sports, 9, 12, 47, 57, 59
  see also boxing
sports equipment room at Kinchela, 33–4, 36–7
spray-painting, 91, 92, 102
spraying kangaroo hides, 109
stealing, *see* robbery

step-father, 72–3, 79
Stockton hospital, 134, 136
stockwhips, 19, 44, 57
Stolen Generations, apology and compensation to, 154
Sunrise Station, 2
Surry Hills, 91

tall ships protest, 120
Taree, 2, 3, 19, 125
  Lilly and Lilly's family, 79, 80–1, 82, 103–4
  Purfleet Mission, 1–9, 11, 50–1, 160
Telfour, Mr (teacher at Kinchela), 29–30, 47, 60
The Block, *see* Redfern and The Block
Thurden, Charlie, 87, 95
Tomago, 78, 79
Toronto, 127
toys, 12
  at Kinchela, 56
traditional lifestyle, 2, 3–5, 6
Trial Bay Gaol, 57
trustee system, Kinchela, 24
'Turrumbumdeen', 2

uncles, 6, 69–73, 77–8, 81, 100
  Dan, 78, 85, 86
  Gary, 77
  Gilbert, 76, 77, 135, 136
  Kevin, 76, 77, 135
  Nate, 77
  Nick, 76
  Ray, 9
  Shane, 11, 100, 101, 104
  see also Simon, Uncle Jim
United Aborigines Mission, 2

United Pentecostal Church, Mount Druitt, 101–2, 103, 104–5, 108–9

violence, 65, 80, 83, 93
  armed robbery, 68, 93–4
  Bill's father's attitude towards, 12
  on The Block, 121, 137, 139–40; after T J Hickey's death, 144–5
  in jail, 95
  see also aggression; bashings; fights; punishment at Kinchela
visitors to Kinchela, 34, 51, 56

'Walkin' down the line', 35–7
Wallaga Lake, 3
watch given to Maitland Jail prisoner, 131–2
welfare department, 59, 63, 64
  see also Aborigines Welfare Board
Wellington, 68–73, 74, 76–7
Welsh, Ray, 138
wet beds, 22, 24, 27, 28–9, 45
wet pants, 19
whips, 19, 44, 57
Wickham, 86–8
Windale, 127–8
women, relationships with, *see* relationships with women
Woolloomooloo, 150
work, *see* employment
work boys, 30–1, 34, 35, 60, 61, 135
  dairy work, 24, 27, 57
Worthington, Mr, 58, 59, 61, 62, 63
Wyong, retreat at, 131–2

'yarni', 92–4
youth leader, 101

First published in 2009
by Aboriginal Studies Press

© William Simon, Des Montgomerie and Jo Tuscano, 2009

All rights reserved. No part of this book may be reproduced or transmitted in any form or by any means, electronic or mechanical, including photocopying, recording or by any information storage and retrieval system, without prior permission in writing from the publisher. The *Australian Copyright Act 1968* (the Act) allows a maximum of one chapter or 10 per cent of this book, whichever is the greater, to be photocopied by any educational institution for its education purposes provided that the educational institution (or body that administers it) has given a remuneration notice to Copyright Agency Limited (CAL) under the Act.

Aboriginal Studies Press
is the publishing arm of the
Australian Institute of Aboriginal
and Torres Strait Islander Studies.
GPO Box 553, Canberra, ACT 2601
Phone: (61 2) 6246 1183
Fax: (61 2) 6261 4288
Email: asp@aiatsis.gov.au
Web: www.aiatsis.gov.au/aboriginal_studies_press

National Library of Australia Cataloguing-In-Publication data:

Author: Simon, Bill, 1960–

Title: Back on the block : Bill Simon's story / Bill Simon, Des Montgomerie, Jo Tuscano.

ISBN: 9780855756772 (pbk.)

Notes: Includes index.

Subjects: Simon, Bill, 1960-
Aboriginal Australians — Biography. Aboriginal Australians — New South Wales — Redfern — Biography. Stolen generations (Australia) — Biography.

Other Authors/Contributors: Montgomerie, Des. Tuscano, Jo.

Dewey Number: 305.89915092

Printed in Australia by Ligare Pty Ltd

Cover images: Bill Simon ministering on The Block, Redfern, Sydney